ROOTS & ROUTES

The Language of Life

Gary Wilson

INTRODUCTION

Initiatives is about language – what it is, what it does and where it comes from.

This Resourcebook is arranged in units, each of which looks in detail at one aspect of language. Tapes and photocopy repromasters run alongside each unit, and together they present a range of options to choose from, which may include:

- discussion in large or small groups
- role playing
- drafting your own response in writing
- presenting findings to the group as a whole
- experimenting with new forms of writing
- making radio programmes
- interviewing people in the community
- research and analysis
- looking at paintings
- responding to poetry and prose
- thinking about accent and dialect
- questioning your own assumptions about language and people.

Some of the activities you will be invited to tackle may be quite difficult. Don't be put off by your first response; use that response and build on it – share it with other members of the group, talk about it with your teacher, discuss it at home. Your ideas and feelings are crucial in coming to an understanding of how language works.

Whatever you're investigating, **share** your ideas, **comment** on each other's opinions, **follow up** new ideas that occur to you – above all, use your own **initiative!**

CONTENTS

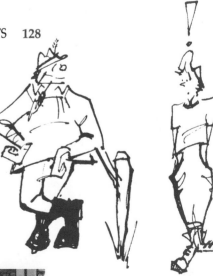

OPENING UP

Every individual in every classroom has a different background, and language forms a very important part of that background. How we talk – the language, the accents, the dialects we use – how much our families read and what we read or even how much we write, for pleasure or other purposes, varies considerably from family to family. In other words we all have different roots. *Thinking about our future involvement with language shows us that we all may also be taking very different* routes. *One thing is certain: language is all-important in our day-to-day lives.*

A Few Questions . . .

● To begin to focus your attention on this issue, listen to the tape extracts of young people and teachers discussing these and other questions about language:

What type of writing do you find most enjoyable?

Do you like being read to?

Do you often switch off when a teacher talks to you?

How do you feel when your work is displayed on the wall?

Do your parents read more than you?

Do teachers talk too much?   Do students talk too much?

Have you ever had a piece of writing in a school magazine?

Do you have a lot of books at home?

Do you enjoy discussions?

Have you ever worried about spelling?

Do you read for pleasure at home?

Were you read to at home before you started school?

What's the best/worst kind of English lesson?

Is your handwriting a problem?

Do you like project work?

Do you always check your work through?

Do you like the way you talk?

Do you like being given a title for a piece of writing?

How do you feel when a teacher reads out your work?

What do you think about poetry?

Do you use a dictionary or thesaurus?

Do you always read through a teacher's comments on your work?

Do you feel that certain types of books are better than others?

Do you have to write too much?

Do you ever feel you could write more?

Are you a good listener?

Do you like a teacher to correct work in red ink?

Do you write for pleasure at home?

How do you feel about reading aloud or talking in front of the class?

What are the hardest things you have to read?

Do you like copying things up neatly?

What did you like best about writing in your infant and junior schools?

What are you likely to be doing as far as language is concerned in future study/employment/leisure? (Reading/writing/talking?)

What do you still need to learn?

Options

● Listen to the people on the tape discussing their experience with language. How familiar are their comments? Do members of your group experience similar things?

● Tape an interview with a partner about their experience of language and how they see their future involvement with language. Piece together from the ideas above and from ideas of your own a list of questions, in a suitable order, for the script for the interview.

● As a group of three produce a questionnaire designed to collect information about the whole year group's experience of language. One of you could take 'Talking', another 'Reading' and the other 'Writing'. Write up your findings as a report afterwards.

● Write up the interview, or the results of the questionnaire, as an article for a student newspaper. What are your conclusions about how people are involved with language at school? What are the positive and negative issues?

What Does It All Mean?

The most familiar language in our lives consists of our own names and the names of the places familiar to us, but we are often very ignorant about what they actually mean.

What does your first name mean?
What does your surname mean?
Does your house have a name? What does it mean?
What does the name of your street mean?
What does the name of your village/area mean?
What does the name of your town mean?
What do you mean, you don't know?

On the next two pages, and on Repromaster 1*, are three very basic guides to the meanings of names (libraries have far more).*

Options

● Discover all you can about your name, and local street and place names. If your name originated in another country, investigate its original meaning by asking your family or using the library. Examine a map of the area around your school to work out as many meanings of place names as you can by using the list on page 9.

● Write out your name and address using the original meanings you have discovered. Write out your journey to school using the definitions as the example below shows (if you travel with friends, you'll need definitions of their names too). Or write directions for someone to get to your house using the original meanings of street and place names. The tone of your piece of writing should sound quite ancient as you are, after all, going back many many years to discover the origin of the names. Your history teacher may be able to help here. Very old maps might be useful too.

> Benjamin Wilson set off for school. He had to set out for Sheffield early. He left Gilltop Farm, and walked down Smithy Lane. He walked into the village. . .

> The first born son of William set off for school. He had to set out for the ancient sheep pasture early. He left the farm at the valley top and walked down the road where the blacksmith once worked. He walked into the village..

● Whilst you're finding out about names you could also find out why your parents chose your name. What name(s) would you have chosen for yourself? What names might you choose for your own children? Many older people do still believe that names fit faces and that there is such a thing as a 'typical' Fred. Ask your parents if they have such ideas. Report your findings to the class.

● What about the more friendly pet names your family use towards each other? How did they come about? Report your findings to the class.

● Discover if anyone calls their parents by their first names. Does it make any difference? Would it to you?

● Talk about nicknames. Where did people's nicknames originate? If someone in the class is unhappy about theirs, be kind — you could even find a pleasanter one for them.

ORIGINS

Surnames Reflecting Medieval Life

Archer a professional archer, or perhaps a champion.
Arrowsmith responsible for making arrow-heads.

Bacchus a worker in the bakehouse.
Backer a baker.
Bacon he would have sold or prepared bacon.
Bailey a bailiff, a word that described (high) officials of several kinds.
Baker the bread-maker.
Barber he trimmed beards, cut hair, pulled out teeth and performed minor operations.
Barker he worked with bark for the leather trade.
Bayliss usually the son of a *Bailey*.
Baxter a female baker.
Bowman like *Archer*.
Brasher a brazier, brass-founder.
Brewer occasionally from a place name, but usually what it says.
Brewster a female brewer.
Butcher as now, though once a dealer in buck's (goat's) flesh.
Butler chief servant who supervised the bottles.
Campion a professional fighter, a champion.
Carpenter as now.
Carter driver, perhaps maker, of carts.
Cartwright maker and repairer of carts.
Carver a sculptor.
Castle(man) man employed at the castle.
Catchpole sheriff's official who seized poultry in lieu of debts.
Cater purveyor of goods to a large household.
Century belt-maker.
Chafer worker at a lime-kiln.
Chaffer merchant.
Chalker white-washer.
Challender seller of blankets.
Challinor as *Challender*.
Chalmers as *Chambers*.
Chamberlain once a nobleman's personal servant, but became a general factotum in an inn.
Chambers as *Chamberlain*.
Champion see *Campion*.
Chandler he made or sold candles.
Chaplin a chaplain.
Chapman at first a merchant, later a pedlar.
Chaundler as *Chandler*.

Clark(e) a minor cleric.
Coke a cook.
Collier he sold charcoal.
Cook(e) a professional cook. The extra 'e' acquired accidentally in such names or an attempt to disguise the name's meaning.
Cooper concerned with wooden casks, buckets, etc.
Cowper as *Cooper*.
Day often a worker in a dairy.
Draper maker and seller of woollen cloth.
Dyer a cloth-dyer. Dye was deliberately changed from die to avoid confusion.
Falconer in charge of the falcons, used for hunting.
Falkner, Faulkner, etc as *Falconer*.
Farmer the modern meaning came after the surname. He was a tax-collector before that, 'farm' once meaning 'firm or fixed payment'.
Farrar a smith or farrier.
Fearon an ironmonger or smith.
Feather a dealer in feathers.
Fisher a fisherman.
Fletcher he made and sold arrows.
Forester a gamekeeper.
Forster sometimes a cutler, scissors-maker, or as *Forester*.
Fowler a hunter of wild birds.
Frobisher he polished swords, armour and the like.
Fuller he 'fulled' cloth, cleansing it.
Gardner, Gardiner, etc a gardener.
Glover a maker and seller of gloves.
Goldsmith often a banker as well as a goldsmith.
Grave a steward.
Grieve manager of property, a bailiff.
Harper maker or player of harps.
Hayward literally a 'hedgeguard'. In charge of fences and enclosures.
Herd a herdsman.
Hooper he fitted hoops on casks and barrels.
Hunt, Hunter both huntsman.
Kellogg literally 'kill hog', a slaughterer.
Kemp as *Campion*.

Knight in the Middle Ages the meaning was 'a military servant'.

Lander a launderer.

Lavender a launderer.

Leach a doctor.

Leadbeater, Leadbetter, Leadbitter, etc worker in lead.

Leech a doctor.

Lister a dyer of cloth.

Lorimer a spur-maker.

Machin a mason, stoneworker.

Marchant a merchant.

Marshall a marshal, originally in charge of horses, rising to be a high official.

Mason a skilled stoneworker.

Mercer a dealer in silks and such-like fabrics.

Merchant a dealer, especially wholesale imports/exports.

Mills a miller.

Miller a corn miller.

Milner as *Miller*.

Mulliner as *Miller*.

Naylor a maker and seller of nails.

Page a minor male servant.

Paget a little *Page*.

Paige as *Page*.

Parker keeper of a private park.

Parson a parson, rector.

Parsons servant or son of the Parson.

Pepper a dealer in pepper and other spices.

Piper a pipe-player, but may include the name *Pepper*.

Plummer a plumber, lead-worker.

Potter a maker and seller of earthenware.

Proctor a 'procurator', a steward, agent, tithe-farmer.

Redman sometimes from 'reed-man', a thatcher.

Reeve a high-ranking official, a bailiff, a steward.

Saddler a saddle-maker.

Salter a salt-worker, or seller of salt.

Sargent a domestic, legal, or military servant.

Sawyer a sawer of wood.

Shepherd, Sheppard, etc a shepherd.

Singer a professional singer.

Skinner a preparer of skins, a tanner.

Slater a slate-layer.

Slatter as *Slater*.

Smith a metal-worker, maker of all-important weapons and implements.

Smithers son of *Smith*.

Smythe as *Smith*.

Spencer a dispenser of provisions, a steward or butler.

Spicer a seller of spices.

Spooner a spoon-maker, or roofing-shingle maker.

Squire a knight's attendant, usually a young man of good birth.

Steele a steel-worker.

Stringer a maker of strings for bows.

Tanner a tanner of hides.

Taylor a maker of clothes, though the Normans could also 'tailor' other materials, such as stone.

Thatcher 'thatch' is linked with the Roman 'toga' and means 'to cover'.

Thrower a potter.

Tiller farmer.

Tillman tile-maker or farmer.

Todd foxhunter.

Toddman officially-appointed foxhunter.

Toller toll-collector.

Trainer trapper.

Tranter waggoner.

Trapp trapper.

Travers tollbridge-keeper.

Trinder wheelmaker.

Trotter messenger.

Tucker a cloth-worker.

Turner a wood-worker, but possibly a turnspit-operator, a translator, competitor in tournaments, etc.

Tyler maker and layer of tiles.

Vickers son or servant of a vicar.

Wainwright a waggon-maker and repairer.

Walker a cloth-worker, who trod cloth in order to cleanse it.

Waller sometimes a builder of walls, but other origins possible.

Ward a watchman, guard.

Weaver, Webb, Webber, Webster all mean weaver.

Wheeler a maker of wheels.

Woodward a forester.

Wright a workman who made a variety of articles.

Place Names

Breck hill.

Bridge a crossing place.

By village.

Chester, caster, cester a fortified place.

Combe valley.

Cott, cot, cotte cottage or place of shelter.

Dale valley.

Den a valley or a place where animals were grazed.

Don a hill.

Fell a hill.

Field open place (eg Sheffield – a place for pasturing sheep).

Ford a crossing place.

Gill a valley.

Ham a meadow, a home place, a village.

Hay an enclosure in a forest clearing.

Head implies (sometimes) ancient religious link eg Gateshead – a ritual associated with a goat.

Ing, ingham the followers of (eg Reading – the place of the followers of Reada; Walsingham – the place of the followers of Waels).

Lake water, usually fed by a stream.

Lan, llan a place associated with a saint (used as a prefix).

Leigh, ley, lay an open space.

Port a market place.

Scale a hut.

Slack a valley.

Spital a hospital, a place for lepers.

Stock, stoke a place.

Stow a holy place eg Felixstowe – the holy place of St Felix.

Street a road, a paved way. This may be used as a prefix (streat, strat) eg Stratford, Streeton.

Tarn small lake.

Thorpe hamlet.

Thwaite clearing.

Toft homestead.

Ton, tun farm or manor.

Tre a farm (usually a prefix).

Well a place with a spring.

Wick (inland) buildings, often a farm with cows.

Wick (coastal) a bay.

Worthy an enclosure round a house.

THE LANGUAGE OF LIFE

Opening Up – Language Diary

If you were really to take notice of the activities you involve yourself in during an average day, you would be very surprised at the number of ways you use language. From reading breakfast cereal packets in the morning to a book in bed at night, from arguing with a brother or sister to reading a part in a play at school, from writing a note to a friend in class to writing answers in the Maths GCSE examination – language plays a huge and complex part in your life.

Options

● Using *Repromasters 2* and *3*, keep a language diary for a week. Try to fill it in as fully and as accurately as you possibly can.

● Compare your language diary with a partner's. Discuss the differences. Share your thoughts with the rest of the class.

● Compile a chart of class statistics of hours spent listening to the radio, watching television and reading. Write up the findings.

● What kind of language diary would you imagine your teacher might produce? What about a parent? A doctor? A farmer? Fill in imaginary diaries – or get adults to volunteer.

Anecdotes

Each and every one of us has stories to tell about events in our own lives. The sad fact is that many of us feel that none of these stories are interesting or worth repeating. Many authors, by working on the simplest of ideas, create very enjoyable and readable stories. Have a go yourself – begin by talking about them first.

Options

● Discuss with a partner some of the highlights and unusual incidents that have happened to you during your school days. Take it in turns and keep your anecdotes short.

Decide between you which anecdote would make the best story when written down. Discuss the one that each of you is going to write about and give each other ideas on how to improve it.

Tape the selected anecdotes before you write them down.

Write your story down – asking for help and opinions whenever necessary.

Compare the taped version and the written version.

Join with another pair when you have all finished and share your stories.

● Compare the two versions of the same anecdote below. (A) is from the play version of *Kes* and (B) is from the original novel, *A Kestrel for a Knave* by Barry Hines.

A ANDERSON: Well it was once when I was a kid. I was at junior school, I think, or somewhere like that, and went down to Fowlers Pond, me and this other kid. Reggie Clay they called him, he didn't come to this school; he flitted and went away somewhere. Anyway it was Spring, tadpole time, and it's swarming with tadpoles down there in Spring. Edges of the pond are all black with them, and me and this other kid started to catch them. It was easy, all you did, you just put your hands together and scooped a handful of water up and you'd got a handful of tadpoles. Anyway we were mucking about with them, picking them up and chucking them back and things, and we were on about taking some home, but we'd no jam jars. So this kid, Reggie, says, 'Take your wellingtons off and put some in there, they'll be all right 'til you get home.' So I took them off and we put some water in them and then we started to put taddies in them. We kept ladling them in and I said to this kid, 'Let's have a competition, you have one wellington and I'll have the other, and we'll see who can get most in!' So he started to fill one wellington and I started to fill the other. We must have been at it hours, and they got thicker and thicker, until at the end there was no water left in them, they were just jam packed with tadpoles. You ought to have seen them, all black and shiny, right up to the top. When we'd finished we kept dipping our fingers into them and whipping them up at each other, all shouting and excited like. Then this kid said to me, 'I bet you daren't put one on.' And I said, 'I bet you daren't.' So we said we'd put one on each. We wouldn't though, we kept reckoning to, then running away, so we tossed up and him who lost had to do it first. And I lost, oh, and you'd to take your socks off as well. So I took my socks off, and I kept looking at this wellington full of tadpoles, and this kid kept saying, 'Go on then, you're frightened, you're frightened.' I was as well. Anyway I shut my eyes and started to put my foot in. Oooo, it was just like putting your feet into live jelly. They were frozen. And when my foot went down, they all came over the top of my wellington and when I got my foot to the bottom, I could feel them all squashing about between my toes. Anyway, I'd done it, and I says to this kid, 'You put yours on now.' But he wouldn't, he was dead scared, so I put it on instead. I'd got used to it then, it was all right after a bit; it sent your legs all excited and tingling like. When I'd got them both on I started to walk up to this kid, waving my arms and making spook noises; and as I walked they all came squelching over the tops again and ran down the sides. This kid looked frightened to death, he kept looking down at my wellingtons so I tried to run at him and they all spurted up my legs. You ought to have seen him. He just screamed out and ran home roaring. It was funny feeling though when he'd gone; all quiet, with nobody there, and up to the knees in tadpoles.

B   "Well it was once when I was a kid. I was at Junior school, I think, or somewhere like that, and went down to Fowlers Pond, me and this other kid. Reggie Clay they called him, he didn't come to this school; he flitted and went away somewhere. Anyway it was Spring, tadpole time, and it's swarming with tadpoles down there in Spring. Edges of t'pond are all black with 'em, and me and this other kid started to catch 'em. It was easy, all you did, you just put your hands together and scooped a handful of water up and you'd got a handful of tadpoles. Anyway we were mucking about with 'em, picking 'em up and chucking 'em back and things, and we were on about taking some home, but we'd no jam jars. So this kid, Reggie says, 'Take thi wellingtons off and put some in there, they'll be all right 'til tha gets home.' So I took 'em off and we put some water in 'em and then we started to put taddies in 'em. We kept ladling 'em in and I says to

this kid, 'Let's have a competition, thee have one welli' and I'll have t'other, and we'll see who can get most in!' So he started to fill one welli' and I started to fill t'other. We must have been at it hours, and they got thicker and thicker, until at t'end there was no water left in 'em, they were just jam packed wi' taddies.

"You ought to have seen 'em, all black and shiny, right up to t'top. When we'd finished we kept dipping us fingers into 'em and whipping 'em up at each other, all shouting and excited like. Then this kid says to me, 'I bet tha daren't put one on.' And I says, 'I bet tha daren't.' So we said we'd put one on each. We wouldn't though, we kept reckoning to, then running away, so we tossed up and him who lost had to do it first. And I lost, oh, and you'd to take your socks off an' all. So I took my socks off, and I kept looking at this welli' full of taddies, and this kid kept saying, 'Go on then, tha frightened, tha frightened.' I was an' all. Anyway I shut my eyes and started to put my foot in. Oooo. It was just like putting your feet into live jelly. They were frozen. And when my foot went down, they all came over t'top of my wellington, and when I got my foot to t'bottom, I could feel 'em all squashing about between my toes.

"Anyway I'd done it, and I says to this kid, 'Thee put thine on now.' But he wouldn't, he was dead scared, so I put it on instead. I'd got used to it then, it was all right after a bit; it sent your legs all excited and tingling like. When I'd got 'em both on I started to walk up to this kid, waving my arms and making spook noises; and as I walked they all came squelching over t'tops again and ran down t'sides. This kid looked frightened to death, he kept looking down at my wellies so I tried to run at him and they all spurted up my legs. You ought to have seen him. He just screamed and ran home roaring.

"It was a funny feeling though when he'd gone; all quiet, with nobody there, and up to t'knees in tadpoles."

Options

● Examine the words and phrases that have been changed. Why have they been changed, do you think? Which version is closest to a story being spoken out loud?

● Compare your own written anecdote with your taped version: are there any changes you might make to make it more realistic?

The story of your family background is unique and of great importance to your own life and identity, as well as being fascinating to others. Conduct a detailed exploration of your 'roots'.

Using all the language skills at your disposal, trace the history of your family and preserve it for posterity.

Options

● Discuss with your group what you know of your family's history. Suggest to each other particular areas of interest that you feel should be followed up and written about.

● Talk to your family about your family history. Get them to go back as far in time as they can. Together with your family, draw up a family tree to use for reference throughout the project.

● Listen to or tape anecdotes from older relatives about particular occasions and events of special importance in your family's past, together with any stories about the exploits of particular characters in your family's history. Were there any adventurers or eccentrics? Artists or soldiers? Sportspeople or writers? What was life like for your family during the war? At the time of your birth? In Victorian times? The twenties? During the sixties? Has your family had periods of notable luck or misfortune?

● Write to branches of the family abroad or in far flung corners of Britain. They may have interesting stories to tell.

● Read/research old school reports, letters, postcards, documents, newspaper cuttings, diaries, old photographs, birth, marriage and death certificates. Compile lists of statistics (height, colour of hair, ages, jobs, etc). Photograph birthplaces or old family homes.

● Select the most useful stories and documentation that will help you piece together details of characters and events in your family's past.

● Plan your account so that it is not simply going to be a list of events and characters one after another.

● Review with your family the accuracy of details and descriptions.

● Write the account of your family's history, using anecdotes and detailed descriptions to bring your characters and story alive and grasp the reader's attention.

● Redraft as necessary, seeking the further opinions of your teacher and friends.

● Illustrate to improve the final presentation, for example by using maps to show your family's movements and the location of family groups, together with your family tree, copies of documents, photographs, charts, statistics and so on. Use the maps(*Repromasters 4* and *5*) and time chart (*Repromaster 6*) to keep a record of your research and improve your final presentation.

● Present the end result either in your best handwriting or by using a word processor or typewriter. You might arrange to have the finished product photocopied and bound. This is an important document, so take great care in its production and final presentation. Keep a notebook throughout the process to jot down your thoughts and feelings about what you discover, and include this in the final write-up if appropriate.

OPENING UP

Options

● Working individually or in small groups, make a list of as many different types of writing as you can; for example, think of news stories, poetry, sports reports and so on.

Arrange your list in what you regard as their order of importance.

Write a sentence about the kind of person who would write each item on your list.

Compare your list with those of the rest of the class. Try to agree on an order of importance and select the best description of the kind of person who writes each item.

Discuss the end result. Was it easy to agree on an order of importance? Where do school essays come on the list? Why? Going by the descriptions of the type of writer each item is associated with, how many of the items on the list do you think you might realistically write in your lifetime? Why? What are your conclusions?

● Select one type of writing from your class list and one totally mismatched description of the writer (the crazier the combination the better ... a children's comic writer, writing a sports report?) and produce a short piece of writing, like the one shown. (First of all make a list of typical words that the particular writer might use.)

List of words:-
shine/shone   bright   fine
high pressure depression cloud
shower   storm   lightning
thunder   drift   fog
mild   cold front degrees

Name A. Weather
Form 4B
Form Teacher Mr. Bambrook

After a bad start to the year, weather really has begun to pick up, particularly during the Autumn term.
He certainly began to shine during the examinations and periods of high pressure seem to agree with him.

The outlook for weather is fine, provided of course that he remains consistent. He must not allow his mind drift nor let himself be affected by fits of depression. He has allowed things to cloud the issue in the past, but now he has removed himself from that troublesome shower of boys in the fifth year, who spent most of the time thundering up and down the corridors, he will hopefully be far more settled.

WARM UPS

You could just try a series of these for a lesson on 'persuasion' or 'arguments' or just for fun. Favourites could be used as warm-ups for some of the roleplay exercises and improvisations that you will find throughout the book.
If you can, record some of these activities, listen carefully to the language and see if you can identify any interesting features.

Options

Talkdown

● With a partner, on a given signal, talk both at the same time about a particular topic (an easy one is 'What I did at the weekend', but you might like to try something more adventurous) for thirty seconds. The aim is not to listen to a single word your partner is saying. Look each other in the eye the whole time.

Faulty Goods

● In pairs: one returns a faulty article to the complaints desk of a big store claiming that it doesn't work. The other has to handle the complaint. Try something out-of-the-ordinary like a comb, for example.

Gobbledegook

● Using only made-up words, or using numbers or letters, explain to a partner what sort of day you've had or tell them a joke, tell them a secret or tell them about something you watched on video last night.

Describe an Object

● In pairs: one describes an object whilst the other attempts to draw it.

...in fact,... it's really quite beautiful

Communicate

● Hold a conversation sitting back to back or with eyes closed. Or give directions to a total stranger on how to get to a room at the far end of school, without using your hands or any gestures at all.

Word Associations/Word Disassociations

● The first person starts with a noun; their partner must then quickly say a word that has an association with the previous word. Alternatively, try to find a word which has no connection whatsoever with the previous one.

Oneup

● Try to outdo your partner with lies that gradually become more and more outrageous. Begin by talking about how much spending money you get, or something equally modest.

Put Off

● One person has to tell a story on a given subject – their partner has to interrupt by asking questions that are totally unrelated to the subject. The first person has to answer the questions and then return to the original subject.

True/False

● With a partner: one asks questions, the other answers. Every other answer must be a lie. If the liar laughs or hesitates he/she is out and then you must change places.

Harmony and Discord

● In fours, each taking on the role of a member of a family, sit around a breakfast table. Calmly, and very politely, enact a typical family breakfast scene. Upon an arranged signal from your teacher change the mood dramatically; then, upon the same signal, return to peace and tranquility, and so on. Don't resort to violence! Just use tone of voice and an appropriate choice of words (keep it clean) to indicate whether you are portraying 'harmony' or 'discord'.

Storycircle

● Using only one word each, create a story round a circle. You can play a similar game using a book: each person, when the book is handed to them, is to continue a story begun by the teacher, by adding a sentence then passing the book to the next person.

Snowball

● Half the class should go to one end of the room and the other half to the other end. Each side must make imaginary snowballs, then throw them at the other shouting out a word (any word – except rude ones of course) as each snowball leaves their hands. (Do it quickly.)

One Minute Please

● One person is chosen at random to give a talk for one minute on a given subject (Dirty socks? Matchboxes?) and if that person (a) pauses, (b) repeats anything or (c) goes off the point, another member of the class can challenge them (by shouting "Hesitation!" for example) and continue talking on the subject until the minute is up or until they are challenged . . . and so on.

Yes/No Interlude

● One member of the class must sit in the middle of the circle and answer questions from the teacher and/or the rest of the class for one minute without saying 'yes' or 'no'. If they do use either word, then they are 'out' and it is someone else's turn.

Freeze/Action

● The whole class walks around the classroom and, on a given signal from the teacher, each member of the class starts a conversation with the person nearest them, beginning with the phrase, "Excuse me, but haven't I seen you somewhere before?" Keep talking until you are given another signal; then circulate again . . . and so on.

Whispers

● The class sits in a circle and the teacher whispers a message to the next person on her/his right and so on until the message returns. Compare the original message with the final message.

Rules

● One volunteer leaves the room. The rest of the class meanwhile invents a rule, for example, "All girls answer questions from the volunteer beginning with the word 'well'." The volunteer has to deduce the rule by asking questions.

Fast Thinking

● The group sits in a circle, with a volunteer in the middle. The group passes round an object and the volunteer (with eyes closed) says "Stop" and chooses a letter. Whoever was caught with the object has to think of five nouns and five adjectives beginning with that letter before the object returns to them as it is passed around the circle again.

Mock Interview

● A volunteer leaves the room and the rest of the group thinks up an unusual job for them; the volunteer then returns and the class 'interviews' him/her for that job by asking questions. The group's questions must be a reasonably sensible attempt to discover the volunteer's suitability but mustn't give the game away. The volunteer must answer the questions and when she/he feels sure of what the job is, she/he must say, "Yes, I would like a job as a . . ."

Telephone

● The group sits in a circle, with a telephone in the middle. The teacher indicates that there is someone on the other end for a member of the group. The only other instruction is that it is a very important phone call. Whoever is selected then has to improvise a conversation (leaving the appropriate gaps) with the 'person on the other end'.

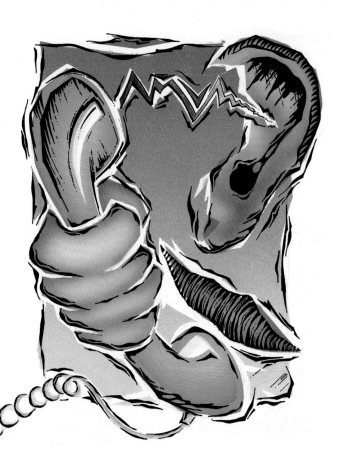

WORD FUN

Options

● Produce dictionary definitions for the 'words' above. Take an action comic' and collect similar examples and produce a short dictionary for 'action comic' readers.

● Have you noticed that many words beginning with Sl— have unpleasant meanings? Check it out in a dictionary. Many words beginning with Wr— seem to be connected with some kind of physical action. (The suggestion is that *Wr!* is close to the sound we make when we are physically exerting ourselves!) Check it out in a dictionary. While you're there have a look at Squ— ,Fl— and Sn—. Do the words with these beginnings have anything in common? Try out some other beginnings – see if you can make even more discoveries.

● Write a sentence (or two or three) in which each word begins with each letter of the alphabet, in the correct order. Here is an example:
"Able bodied conscientious dustmen emptying filthy garbage handle indescribable junk; kitchen leftovers make noxious odours producing quite revolting stenches. This unwholesome vegetation won't exactly yield zeal." (Yes, you can cheat with 'x'.)

● List all this year's fashionable words and produce a dictionary page to help an historian one hundred years from now understand a little more about life today and the language we use.

● Working in groups of three, using a good dictionary, select unusual words. Make a note of the dictionary definition, then write two alternative definitions for each. Now compete against another group. Take a word at a time. The team whose word is being examined reads out the original definition and the two invented ones. Should the opposing team work out which is the correct definition then they gain a point – if not, then the team giving the definitions gains a point.

● Produce a dictionary page with ironic, sarcastic or just plain stupid definitions. These examples from *The Devil's Dictionary* and *The Modern Newspeak* might help.

Urchin	the lower part of a woman's face.
Violin	a bad hotel.
Boomerang	what you say when you frighten a meringue.
Pedestrian	nuisance to traffic, one obstinately re-fusing to travel continuously on wheels.
School Leaver	complete idiot, tiresome statistic.
Self-made	pig ignorant.
Supermarket	corner store in which the customer performs services formerly undertaken by the shopkeeper.

Invention

We see around us many unusual and original examples of language use, from nonsense verse to advertisements, from children's TV characters to jokes. More seriously, writers such as J. R. R. Tolkien have invented new worlds with their own languages. George Orwell invented his own language of the future for the book 1984 and Anthony Burgess invented a futuristic slang for his characters in the science fiction novel A Clockwork Orange. There are many more examples.

Options

● Make a collection of as many examples as you can of this creative use of language.

● Have a go at a little invention yourself: invent names for your school corridors – you could even make signs and seek permission for their display. Some teachers might even agree to having names for their classrooms!

Language is quite heavily dependent on environment – the more something features in your surroundings, the more it will feature in your language. The most famous example of this is the word 'snow' in the Eskimo language: while English has only 'snow' (with 'slush' as a slight variant) Eskimo has a variety of different words – for falling snow, snow on the ground, snow packed hard like ice, etc. And the Australian Aboriginal language of Pintupi has at least ten different words for hole:

yarla	a hole in an object
pirti	a hole in the ground
pirnki	a hole formed by a rock shelf
kartalpa	a small hole in the ground
yulpilpa	a shallow hole in which ants live
mutara	a special hole in a spear
nyarrkalpa	a burrow for small animals
pulpa	a rabbit burrow
makarnpa	a goanna burrow (goanna = an Australian lizard)
katarta	the hole left by a goanna when it has broken the surface after hibernation

● Invent a collection of words that can be used to describe items in your immediate environment. How about new words for homework or teachers, lessons or teachers?

In bygone days shepherds invented their own method of counting sheep. It went like this:
Yahn, Tayn, Tether, Mether, Mumph, Hither, Lither, Auver, Dauver, Dic, Yahndic, Tayndic, Tetherdic, Metherdic, Mumphit, Yahn a Mumphit, Tayn a Mumphit, Tethera Mumphit, Methera Mumphit, Jig It.

● Can you invent your own way of counting to twenty? Notice the use of Yahn (1) in Yahndic (11) (dic = 10).

The pun, or 'play on words', has long been part of English humour. In 1920 Edward Stratemayer invented a particular type of pun, 'Tom Swifties', or Adverbial Puns. Here are two examples.
"I got the first three wrong," she said forthrightly.
"I can't find the oranges," said Tom, fruitlessly.

Another invention that goes back many years involves devising appropriate authors for book titles, eg:
The Housing Problem by Rufus Quick
The Woman Who Sang by Topsy Sharp
Knighted by Watt C. Dunn.

The Reverend W. A. Spooner became famous at the beginning of this century for his invention 'spoonerisms', in which he mixed up the beginnings of words to create a bizarre effect. Can you work out what on earth a 'well boiled icicle' is? How about 'You have hissed my mystery lectures: you have tasted a whole worm. You will leave Oxford on the next town drain.'

Options

● Try inventing your own puns, book titles or spoonerisms. You could even roleplay a conversation in pairs using spoonerisms.

● Catchphrases, slogans and jingles are very modern inventions. Make a collection under various headings, eg game show hosts' catchphrases, radio jingles, soft drink slogans. What makes them successful? Work out what the important ingredients are, then invent some of your own.

● By reworking a well known phrase you could invent for yourself a challenging opening for a story. How about 'Once below a time' or 'Once upon a dream'?

● The crazy inventor Wilf Lunn invented the two machines pictured here. Can you think of ridiculous titles for the machines? Write a brief description of how they function. (Look on the acknowledgements page for the titles which Wilf Lunn himself devised for his inventions.)

● The class needs to divide up into six groups. Each group is given a number from 1 to 6, and an area of the classroom as a base. Your teacher will then distribute the information that each group requires (from *Repromaster 7*). You must then work through the instructions, one at a time, keeping very strictly to the time allowed by your teacher for each activity. Throughout the exercise you must stay in role, acting in the way laid down for your group in the repromaster.

Instructions

1. Read carefully the information about your group. Then, as a group, work out a catchphrase or slogan that expresses very clearly what your group stands for. Write it clearly on the top half of a sticky label.

2. Choose a spokesperson for your group. Add your spokesperson's name to the bottom of the label. Wear your label.

3. A committee, made up of the spokespersons of three of the groups, is going to be elected to decide how the English language will be taught in schools. Decide upon three major points your group wishes to see included in the teaching of English, including details about reading, writing and talking. Remember to take into account what your group stands for. Your spokesperson will soon be competing with others for a place on a committee.

4. Circulate around the room persuading people to vote for your group's spokesperson. Remember, you must stay in role. Make sure all your group has a list of the three points you agreed upon. Everyone has to vote for two candidates in the election. The three who get most votes will form the committee. The one who gets most votes will lead the committee.

5. Your teacher will now distribute the ballot papers which you must fill in secretly.

6. Count the votes.

7. Set up a public meeting where the three elected members of the committee announce the nine points that, between them, they were voted in on. If you can, write up the nine points where everyone can see them. You have now to decide upon *five* main points that you insist will be included in the teaching of English in schools. This must be done in an orderly manner through discussion and by votes taken by a show of hands. Again, stay in role.

The main part of the simulation is now over. Group 3 must now either (a) split up, and one person from that group must join each of the other groups to answer questions; or
(b) make comments as a group in front of the rest of the class.

You may now choose one of the following activities to write up the experience.

● Write about your experience as a member of Group 3.

● Write up your views on the five points that the class finally decided upon.

Voting? Why should I bother?

Words

Out of us all
That make rhymes,
Will you choose
Sometimes –
As the winds use
A crack in a wall
Or a drain,
Their joy or their pain
To whistle through –
Choose me,
You English words?

I know you:
You are light as dreams,
Tough as oak,
Precious as gold,
As poppies and corn,
Or an old cloak:
Sweet as our birds
To the ear,
As the burnet rose
In the heat
Of Midsummer:
Strange as the races
Of dead and unborn:
Strange and sweet
Equally,
And familiar,
To the eye,
As the dearest faces
That a man knows,
And as lost homes are:
But though older far
Than oldest yew, –
As our hills are, old, –
Worn new
Again and again:
Young as our streams
After rain:
And as dear
As the earth which you prove
That we love.
Make me content
With some sweetness
From Wales
Whose nightingales
Have no wings, –
From Wiltshire and Kent
And Herefordshire,
And the villages there, –
From the names, and the things
No less.
Let me sometimes dance
With you,
Or climb
Or stand perchance
In ecstasy,
Fixed and free
In a rhyme,
As poets do.

Edward Thomas

VARIATIONS

Words

But words are things, and a small drop of ink,
    Falling, like dew, upon a thought, produces
That which makes thousands, perhaps millions, think;
    'Tis strange, the shortest letter which man uses,
Instead of speech, may form a lasting link
    Of ages; to what straits old Time reduces
Frail man, when paper – even a rage like this,
Survives himself, his tomb, and all that's his!

Lord Byron, *Don Juan*, *Canto III*

Epilogue

I have crossed an ocean
I have lost my tongue
from the root of the old one
a new one has sprung.

Grace Nichols

Word

The word bites like a fish
Shall I throw it back free
Arrowing to that sea
Where thoughts lash tail and fin?
Or shall I pull it in
To rhyme upon a dish?

Stephen Spender

FINDING A VOICE

BABYTALK

The process of learning language and communication begins before a child is born. Scientists now believe that babies can hear whilst still in the womb and can respond to various sounds, particularly the mother's heartbeat. Babies first communicate at around the age of six weeks when they smile or kick their legs in response to a smile, or some other form of attention. Within a few weeks of that, a baby will add its own sounds to a smile and soon will 'talk' when spoken to. This early form of 'talk' is not an attempt at communication; instead, the baby is simply joining in the game. However, a baby's earliest sounds will often be in a conversational rhythm.

From the age of three months babies will often babble, usually to themselves. Most of the sounds are long vowel sounds such as 'Aaaa' and 'Oooo'. By the age of six months they will sometimes pause whilst adults talk, and then continue to babble – as if they were holding a conversation! Soon they will begin to use two-syllable sounds, 'Aba', 'Booboo', 'Mumum', and so on. By the time babies are about eight months old, they will be paying a lot of attention to adult conversation. If they feel left out they will shout in order to attract notice. This is often the first time they use their voices for real communicative purposes.

Options

● Listen to the tape extract of babytalk and examine the transcript on *Repromaster 9.*

● If you have a young baby in the family, or if one of your neighbours has, tape a sample of the baby's 'talk' and examine it with your group. If possible, follow the development of a baby's language over a period of months and write up your findings.

● Imagine that a baby of eight or nine months could use language like an adult. What might it be saying to itself in a situation such as the one in the picture? (First you'll have to decide what its parents are discussing.) A good way to end your piece of writing might be with the shout mentioned above.

● You might like to try imagining what the baby might be saying to itself whilst being fussed over by relatives at a family Christmas Party, by a grandparent who insists baby has 'Mum's ears', 'Dad's nose' and 'Uncle's smile', by a parent attempting to get a baby to eat at all costs, or during its nightly routine before being put to bed, or whilst stuck in a supermarket trolley. You could even try writing a few days' entries in a baby's diary. Or if the baby in the cartoon were suddenly to reply in an adult voice – you could try writing the conversation that might follow.

● Roleplay a group of babies in pushchairs, discussing in adult voices the way they are constantly fussed over.

● Discuss the way adults use language when talking to babies. Listen to the tape and examine the transcription on *Repromaster 10.* If possible, observe adults talking to a very small baby. What do you notice about the position the adults take and the actions they perform?

More seriously, you might like to try and express, in the form of a piece of poetry or prose, the feelings of a small infant.

Baby Song

From the private ease of Mother's womb
I fall into the lighted room.

Why don't they simply put me back
Where it is warm and wet and black?

But one thing follows on another.
Things were different inside Mother.

Padded and jolly I would ride
The perfect comfort of her inside.

They tuck me in a rustling bed
– I lie there, raging, small, and red.

I may sleep soon, I may forget,
But I won't forget that I regret.

A rain of blood poured round her womb,
But all time roars outside this room.
Thom Gunn

A baby will not use its first 'real' words until the age of about ten or eleven months. Usually these are words for parents, brothers or sisters, pets, and for objects that are important. A baby will then learn words at the rate of several a month until, by the age of two, it will know around two hundred words. By this age a baby will be joining words together. By the age of three a child will be able to hold conversations, which consist largely of questions. Within a few months the toddler will have mastered not only a massive vocabulary but also a wide range of different types of language.

- The various types of language toddlers and small children use are listed below.

- Listen to the tape of a toddler talking and examine the transcript on *Repromaster 11*. What examples of these different types of language can you spot? Use the checklist on *Repromaster 12* to record your findings.

a) "I want" – *getting things done.*
b) "Don't do that" – *being in charge.*
c) "Will you read me" – *getting on with people.*
d) "I'm going to be a digger man" – *being an individual.*
e) "Why?" "What's that?" – *finding out.*
f) "Wouldn't it be funny if . . . ?" "Let's pretend" – *using imagination.*
g) "Let me whisper . . . it's secret" – *passing on information.*

Options

- Find out from your parents what your first words and phrases were. Compare your findings with the rest of the group. Can you find similarities? Are there any words which are more common among boys than among girls – or vice versa? What unusual pronunciations did you come out with? Do any of them still exist within the family as pet names for things?

- With the help of the research above, stories from your parents about your first three years of life, and by using your first drawings and baby photographs, write about the 'you' you can't remember.

GLIMP A TWUZZLE!

This baby, over the next few years, will develop the ability to use language as well as anyone else. It could be any language, depending on the language he hears around him as he grows. He will begin by communicating with simple sounds that gradually become more and more recognisable as adults correct what they hear, and help to shape the baby's sounds into words. Parents will react to the earliest sounds – 'ma-ma-ma' and 'da-da-da', for example – and encourage the baby to connect them to names for his parents. Interestingly, although English uses the word 'mama', French uses 'maman', Swahili 'mama' and Chinese 'mah' for 'mother', the word for 'father' in parts of Russia is 'mama', and the word for 'mother' is 'dada'!

Wherever a baby is born, however, its first words are very similar, and it is the adults around the baby that give the words their meanings. Gradually, through imitation, a baby's language will increase, first with lots of individual words, and then, towards the middle of the baby's second year, pairs of words. By the age of three and a half, most of the rules of English grammar will be understood and a toddler's vocabulary will be huge.

Not all of this process is performed by imitation, however. Studies into language development clearly show that we all naturally possess the ability to understand how words should be put together to make sense. The following experiment with a group of five-year-olds, using imaginary words, shows you exactly what this means:

TEACHER: If this creature is called a frop, what are two of them called?
CHILDREN: Frops.
TEACHER: In this picture the frop is doing something with its feet that we call glumping. What do frops do with their feet?
CHILDREN: They glump.
TEACHER: This frop did the same thing yesterday. Can someone give me a sentence explaining what happened yesterday?
CHILDREN: Yesterday the frop glumped.

● You are, of course, a lot more experienced in language use than these youngsters – but how about trying a similar experiment? With a partner, invent a set of instructions informing people how they can "Glimp a twuzzle in five easy stages", or outline "Ten important points to remember when flopping a doowang". You could devise an illustrated talk for your group or class.

It is, of course, possible to communicate without using proper words at all.

Options

● With a partner, roleplay an argument about some money one of you owes the other. Don't use any words at all, use only the letter 'A'.

● With a partner, work out a series of simple mimes where you produce simple sound effects in order to make the actions easy to understand. Pouring water from a jug, for example, would be accompanied by 'glug glug glug'. Share your ideas with the class.

● Have a look at the sound poems produced by young children, using no words at all – then have a go yourself. See if your group can work out what your poem is about without the help of a title.

The Vending Machine
beep, beep, beep, beep, beep, beep,
clink clonk
blup, blup, blup, blup,
Tocercher, Tocercher
chrrrrrrrrrrrrrr
gulp, gulp, gulp, gulp, gulp.
birrrrrrrrrrp

A Day At The Office
ch, ch, chch, ch, chch
ping
sh
ch, ch, chch, ch, chch
Brr Brr Brr Brr
ting
blub blub blub blub
blub blub
ting ting
tat tat tat
blub blub blub blub

Babysitter
ssshhh
waaar waaar waaar
sshh sshh
waaar waaar waaar
sshh SSHH
waaar WAAAR
SSHHHH
WAAAR
dum di dum dum dum, dum di dum dum . . .

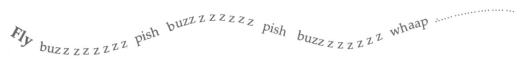

Fly buzz z z z z z z pish buzz z z z z z z pish buzz z z z z z z whaap

READING

Learning to read is a complicated business. To begin with there is the shape of the letters: not just 26 different letters but 43 altogether when you count the change in shape of most letters when capitals are used:

a	b	c	d	e	f	g	h	i	j	k	l	m
A	B		D	E	F	G	H	I	J	K	L	M

n	o	p	q	r	s	t	u	v	w	x	y	z
N			Q		R		T				Y	

The way in which different combinations of letters require different pronunciation can appear totally confusing. How easily can you read this aloud without stumbling?

I take it you already know
Of tough and bough and cough and dough?
Others may stumble but not you,
On hiccough, thorough, laugh and through?
Well done! And now you wish, perhaps,
To learn of less familiar traps?

Beware of heard, a dreadful word
That looks like beard and sounds like bird,
And dead: It's said like bed, not bead –
For goodness sake don't call it 'deed'!
Watch out for meat and great and threat
(They rhyme with suite and straight and debt).

A moth is not a moth in mother
Nor both in bother, broth in brother,
And here is not a match for there
Nor dear and fear for bear and pear,
And then there's dose and rose and lose –
Just look them up – and goose and choose,
And cork and work and card and ward,
And font and front and word and sword,
And do and go and thwart and cart . . .
Anon.

Once we become able readers, however, something very surprising happens – not only do we not read every single word, we literally only need to recognise parts of the letters. Can you read this for example?

Similarly, if we chop words horizontally in half we can also read the original message.

"This baby bed is just right," she shouted loudly, and in no time she fell fast asleep.

Interestingly, it is much easier to understand the message if it is the top half we examine rather than the bottom half.

"This bed is too hard," she cried, and tried the middle-sized bed.

In much the same way we pick up more information from the first half of a word than from the second.

f		is		es		ot		eal		o		ou
I		th		do		nc		app		t		yc

a and he
I in is
it of that
the to was

all as at be but are for had
have him his not on one
said so they we with you 20

about an back been before big by call
came can come could did do down first
from get go has her here if into just like
little look made make me more much
must my no new now off only or our over
other out right see she some their them
then there this two up want well went who
were what when where which will your old 68

After Again Always Am Ask Another Any Away Bad Because Best Bird Black Blue Boy Bring Day Dog Don't Eat Every Fast Father Fell Find Five Fly Four Found Gave Girl Give Going Good Got Green Hand Head Help Home House How Jump Keep Know Last Left Let Live Long Man Many May Men Mother Mr. Never Next Once Open Own Play Put Ran Read Red Room Round Run Sat Saw Say School Should Sing Sit Soon Stop Take Tell Than These Thing Think Three Time Too Tree Under Us Very Walk White Why Wish Work Womah Would Yes Year Bus Apple Baby Bag Ball Bed Book Box Car Cat Children Cow Cup Dinner Doll Door Egg End Farm Fish Fun Hat Hill Horse Jam Letter Milk Money Morning Mrs. Name Night Nothing Picture Pig Place Rabbit Road Sea Shop Sister Street Sun Table Tea Today Top Toy Train Water 150

This area represents 19.750 further words. Space does not permit the printing of these words.

Amongst your group you may, if you attended different infant schools, have been taught to read in a variety of different ways. (You may be interested in visiting your old school to find out how you were taught.) The various approaches include the use of 'Reading Schemes'. The following poem is poking fun at one particular style of book that is sometimes used.

Reading Scheme

Here is Peter. Here is Jane. They like fun.
Jane has a big doll. Peter has a ball.
Look, Jane, look! Look at the dog! See him run!

Here is Mummy. She has baked a bun.
Here is the milkman. He has come to call.
Here is Peter. Here is Jane. They like fun.

Go Peter! Go Jane! Come, milkman, come!
The milkman likes Mummy. She likes them all.
Look, Jane, look! Look at the dog! See him run!

Here are the curtains. They shut out the sun.
Let us peep! On tiptoe Jane! You are small!
Here is Peter. Here is Jane. They like fun.

I hear a car, Jane. The milkman looks glum.
Here is Daddy in his car. Daddy is tall.
Look, Jane, look! Look at the dog! See him run!

Daddy looks very cross. Has he a gun?
Up milkman! Up milkman! Over the wall!
Here is Peter. Here is Jane. They like fun.
Look, Jane, look! Look at the dog! See him run!

Wendy Cope

The poet pokes fun at this particular type of reading scheme because she believes it to be "written in an extraordinary language that no real person would ever speak". The list here is the result of a piece of research to discover the most common words in both children's and adults' speech and in books. The twelve words in the top left hand corner are the twelve most common, and equal a quarter of all language that is commonly used. As the words become smaller on the list their use becomes less common. The famous reading scheme parodied above was based on this list.

Options

● How naturally could you write a short paragraph using the hundred most common words?

● Listen to the taped interview with an adult who has recently learned to read. Discuss their experiences.

● Using the repromaster questionnaire (*Repromaster 13*), conduct your own research amongst your friends, family and teachers about how they learned to read, particularly if you or any of them can read another language.

● Attempt to write a more 'natural' early reading book for children, limiting yourself to the 250 most common words. Keep to a small number of characters (each new name is a new word to learn – thus it becomes more difficult). The most important thing is that both the dialogue and the story itself must be in a very normal style. "They call this little boy Peter" is more natural, for example, than "Here is Peter". If possible try out your story on a young child who is learning to read.

READ ALL ABOUT IT

Reading is an extremely complicated skill, but by your age you probably take it very much for granted, reading everything from the writing on a toilet wall to the details of television programmes in the evening newspaper. We are surrounded by things to read, from timetables to textbooks, from signs to record sleeves. Instructions, notices, letters, labels and magazines, the list is endless – we read them all, almost without thinking. But just how carefully do we read? What goes on in our minds? Try a simple experiment – read the following, quickly:

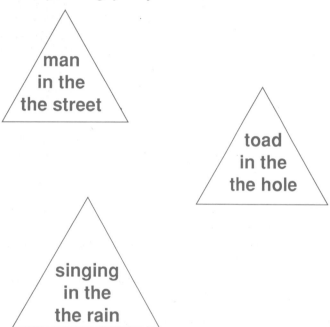

Most people don't realise that in each, one word has been repeated. To a certain extent we read what we think we see and what makes sense to us. Because we don't need all the information on a page, it's quite easy to read something with words missing. Try this:

The new boy at the house   George. He was weird. He used to wobble up and   the road on his bright blue bike, looking   you. His face   very white and his   were staring. He'd   little tufts of hair on his chin. It   me feel strange just to look at him. If I went up to him he would just   still and   at me – his eyes seemed to look right through me so that I wanted to look round and   what it was that he was looking at behind. He never smiled or spoke. Just   . It made me want to   away. He didn't seem able to walk properly   all. His legs seemed to jerk in the middle, with his knees giving a little click with   step he took. And his arms would just hang down, with his fat red   on the end of them as if they had nothing to   with the rest of his body at   . He was always there, wobbling about on his   or clicking down the street, watching us. He   weird.

We make it make sense.

Sometimes, when we come across a word we know has more than one meaning, we have to work a little harder. Read this:

The day on the river started badly. She had tears in her dress from the brambles growing by the riverside. Rowing was something that neither of them had mastered and they rowed about who could do it best. After a minute examination of the map they discovered they were lost. To make matters worse the bows in her hair became entangled in the branches of an overhanging willow tree while they drifted along, and as she struggled to free her hair, the bows of the boat became firmly wedged in the weeds near the bank.

Below, the arrows show how you either had to think back or look ahead before you could make sense of certain words.

The day on the river started badly. She had (tears) in her (dress) from the brambles growing by the riverside. (Rowing) was something that neither of them had mastered and they (rowed) about who could do it best.) After a (minute) (examination) of the map they discovered they were lost. To make matters worse the (bows) in her (hair) became entangled in the branches of an overhanging willow tree while they drifted along, and as she struggled to free her hair, the (bows) of the (boat) became firmly wedged in the weeds near the bank.

● Write a short passage containing as many words with double meanings as you can think of. Get your partner to read it and then put in circles and arrows to 'map out' their reading journey.

● Take a short passage at random from any work the teacher may have available and experiment with the number of words you can remove before it becomes impossible to read.

One of the hardest but most important things to learn when you are reading is to read at a variety of speeds. It would take a long time to find a telephone number if you had to read a directory from cover to cover, for example, and you might end up electrocuting yourself if you don't carefully read every word of a set of instructions! How many, more serious examples of pieces of reading matter that require different speeds of reading can you think of?

● You have 25 seconds to read the following. Working with your group, see how much you remember afterwards.

I went to Julie's and stood waiting for her to change out of her uniform. George was sitting on his step next door, with a gold-fish bowl stuck in front of him. Right, I thought. I'll go and talk to him. I went and stood by him, while he trailed his hand in the gold-fish water.

"What are you doing, George?" I asked. I felt as if I was talking to one of Julie's little brothers.

"I'm catching fish," he said thickly. It was the first time I had ever heard his voice. It wasn't all up and down squeaky like Kevin's is now. It was already nearly like a man's voice. I watched him while he wriggled his fingers about in the bowl, and then he brought a gold-fish out and laid it on the step beside him. It jumped about for a bit, making a clapping sound on the concrete, and then heaved itself heavily sideways, gasping helplessly.

"Put it back, George," I said firmly. "Put it back or it will die."

"No," he said, putting his hands over it and looking up at me defiantly. "It's mine. It's my fish."

Julie came and joined me, and I told her what George had done.

"That's wicked and cruel," she said. "What harm has that fish ever done you?"

"I don't like it," he said. He brought a penknife out of his pocket and flicked it open. He leered up at us. Then he held the fish between his thumb and first finger and very gently and firmly sliced it across with his knife. The fish's cold eye stared up at us. We couldn't say anything, either of us. I'd watched my Mum filleting plaice sometimes, that she'd bought half-alive still off Fish-May's cart down by the slipway – chop the head off, wash the blood out, prise out the bones like a long delicate comb – but I'd never been sickened by that like I was at the sight of this weird lad slicing up his gold-fish. The three of us looked down in silence at the slimy pieces of fish glistening on the steps, and then suddenly Julie said, "Hey George, your mum's coming!"

We turned to run off, as guilty as he, but George's hand streaked out, quick as lightning, picked up the fish pieces, and popped them in his mouth. He stared at us thoughtfully, chewing.
Berlie Doherty, *How Green You Are*

Finish.

How did you do?

One everyday example of when we need to use a wide range of reading skills is the reading of a newspaper or magazine. The way we go about it is a matter of personal taste and individual interest.

Miss Marple gave her attention first to the main news on the front page. She did not linger long on that because it was equivalent to what she had already read this morning, though possibly couched in a slightly more dignified manner. She cast her eye down the table of contents. Articles, comments, science, sport; then she pursued her usual plan, turned the paper over and had a quick run down the births, marriages and deaths, after which she proposed to turn to the page given to correspondence, where she nearly always found something to enjoy; from that she passed on to the Court Circular, on which page today's news from the sale rooms could also be found. A short article on science was often placed there, but she did not propose to read that. It seldom made sense for her.
Agatha Christie, *Nemesis*

What does this description tell you about Miss Marple's personality?

● Try this experiment: using several copies of today's newspapers (tabloids), give yourself ten minutes to read one. As you do so, mark a number on the items with felt tip pen in the order in which you read them.

Then write briefly about your own reading journey, saying why you chose each article (in the same way as Agatha Christie writes about Miss Marple's journey). Why did you choose to read certain items first? Why did you avoid others?

Then discuss your partner's newspaper with her/him and work out what it says about their interests and personality.

Then place all the newspapers in a big pile. Select one at random and, with your partner, discuss the interests of the person who has read that particular newspaper.

● What storyline is suggested by what this character chose to read? (Why is the reader so keen to know the racing results? Does he need money? Is he planning to leave the country? How is this connected to the front-page story? *You* decide.)

● Using today's newspapers number six items at random. Then write a story about the character you have created.

VOICE FROM THE VOICELESS

The winner of the Whitbread Book Prize for 1987, Christopher Nolan, could communicate for the first ten years of his life only by using his eyes and various body signals. He was brain damaged during birth, leaving him without the power of speech or the ability to control the movement of his body. Mentally he was undamaged. In his award-winning autobiography he traced the development of his communication with the outside world. He gave himself the name of Joseph when telling his life story.

He gazed his hurt gaze, lip protruding, eyes busy in conversation. He ordered her to look out the window at the sunshine. He looked hard at her ear ordering her to listen to the birds singing. Then jumping on her knees he again asked her to cock her ear and listen to the village children out at play in the school yard. Now he jeered himself. He showed her his arms, his legs, his useless body. Beckoning his tears he shook his head . . . He was only three years old but he cried the tears of a sad man . . .

. . . Looking through his tears he saw her as she bent low in order to look into his eyes. "I never prayed for you to be born crippled," she said. "I wanted you to be full of life, able to run and jump and talk just like Yvonne. But you are you, you are Joseph not Yvonne. Listen here Joseph, you

can see, you can hear, you can think, you can understand everything you hear, you like your food, you like nice clothes, you are loved by me and Dad. We love you just as you are." Pussing still, snivelling still, he was listening to his mother's voice. She spoke sort of matter-of-factly but he blubbered moaning sounds. His mother said her say and that was that. She got on with her work while he got on with his crying.

The decision arrived at that day was burnt forever in his mind. He was only three years in age but he was now fanning the only spark he saw, his being alive and more immediate, his being wanted just as he was.

The style of communication, using only signals, continued throughout his early years. He became a pupil at a school attached to the Central Remedial Clinic in Dublin. Communication blossomed with others outside his family for the first time.

Such were Joseph's teachers and such was their imagination that the mute boy became constantly amazed at the almost telepathic degree of certainty with which they read his facial expression, eye movements and body language. Many a good laugh was had by teacher and pupil as they deciphered his code. It was at moments such as these that Joseph recognised the face of God in human form. It glimmered in their kindness to him, it glowed in their keenness, it hinted in their caring, indeed it caressed in their gaze.

His frustrations at his inability to express his thoughts, ideas and feelings in words continued to grow. There came a breakthrough at the age of ten.

Writing by hand failed. Typing festered hope. The typewriter was not a plaything. Boy Joseph needed to master it for the good of his sanity, for the good of his soul. Years had taught him the ins and outs of typewriting, but fate denied him the power to nod and hit the keys with his head-mounted pointer. Destruction secretly destroyed his every attempt to nod his pointer onto the keys. Instead great spasms gripped him rigid and sent his simple nod into a farcical effort which ran to each and every one of his limbs.

Eva Fitzpatrick had done years of duty trying to help Joseph to best his body . . .

Now a new drug was being administered to the spastic boy and even though he was being allowed to take only a small segment of Lioresal tablet, he was beginning already to feel different. The little segments of Lioresal tablet seemed harmless, but yet they were the mustard seeds of his and Eva's hours of discovery . . .

Breathing a little easier, his body a little less trembling, he sat head cupped in Eva's hands. He even noticed the scent of her perfume but he didn't glance in the mirror. Perhaps it won't happen for me today he teased himself but he was wrong, desperately, delightfully wrong. Sweetness of certainty sugared his now. Yes, he could type. He could freely hit the keys and he looked in the mirror and met her eyes. Feebly he smiled but she continued to study him. Looking back into her face he tried to get her response, but turning his wheelchair she gracefully glided back along the corridor to his classroom . . .

Of the great discovery Nora knew not and Joseph chose not to tell her. Boyblue bested his body but he bragged but to himself.

"Mrs Meehan, have you seen Joseph at his typing?" innocently enquired Eva Fitzpatrick. "No, Eva, he hasn't been at his typewriter for about eighteen months now," said unwary Nora. Eva smiled in understanding but asked Nora, "Will you come to see him at his next typing lesson?" "Sure," said innocent Nora, "when do you take him again?" "Next Wednesday afternoon at 2.15," said Eva.

Nora sat watching. Spasms ripped through Joseph's body. Sweat stood out on his face. He was trying to let his mother see what he was capable of. She was not impressed. He could see that despite his ordeal. The phone rang and Eva suggested that perhaps Nora would

take over from her and hold Joseph's head. The spasms held him rigid but within a couple of minutes he felt himself relaxing. Nora waited, her son's chin cupped in her hands. Then he stretched and brought his pointer down and typed the letter 'e'. Swinging his pointer to the right he then typed another letter, and another one and another. Eva finished speaking on the telephone and Nora, while still cupping Joseph's chin turned and said, "Eva, I know what you're talking about – Joseph is going for the keys himself – I could actually feel him stretching for them." Eva, his courageous teacher, clenched her fist and brought it down with a bang on the table. "So I was right, I was afraid to say anything, I had to be sure," she said as she broadly smiled.

Joseph sat looking at his women saviours. They chatted about their discovery while he nodded in happy unbelievable bewilderment. He felt himself float reliably on gossamer wings. He hungered no more. He giggled nervously before he even bespoked his thanks. He cheered all the way up the corridor, said goodbye to dear Eva and giggled and cheered up into Nora's face all the way home.

At the age of fourteen the extraordinary fruits of his labours, a collection of poems, were accepted by a publisher.

Slowly she poured and then sort of casual she said, "I had a telephone call from Weidenfeld's. 'Yes, we're interested,' they said, in fact they told me to tell you that they feel privileged to have been allowed to read your work and they would be honoured to publish it." Joseph's whole body reacted, his face looked stunned, his eyes flew heavenwards, a very silence basked round his heart. He searched for a voice to utter words which his mouth framed . . . Now this was his moment of birth, now he had defeated dyed death and bestowed birth to himself. He birthed an author.

VOICE FROM THE VOICELESS

About this collection of poetry, Professor John Carey writes:

He plummeted into language like an avalanche, as if it were his one escape route from death – which, of course, it was. He had been locked for years in the coffin of his body, unable to utter. When he found words he played rapturously with them, making them riot and lark about, echoing, alliterating and falling over one another.

About the autobiographical novel, **Under the Eye of the Clock,** *he writes:*

For this is a voice coming from silence, and a silence that has, as Nolan is aware, lasted for centuries. He has a keen sense of the generations of mute, helpless cripples who have been 'dashed, branded and treated as dross', for want of a voice to tell us what it feels like. Now that voice – or at any rate that redeeming link with a typewriter – has come, and we know. On page after page of this book, Nolan tells us. It should not be possible, after reading it, ever again to think as we have before about those who suffer what he suffers. That is what makes it not just an outstanding book but a necessary one.

Options

● "This was his moment of birth," "he hungered no more," "not just an outstanding book but a necessary one." In groups discuss the phrases quoted above. What do they mean? What other important or powerful phrases can you find?

● Write down what you imagine might have been running through Nora's mind at the moment of breakthrough with her son's typewriting.

● Throughout the book Christie Nolan writes about groups of school children discussing him whilst he is present. Write one of these conversations as you might imagine it.

One sad note in the book is the story told in the following extract, of an American journalist who visits Christie and later publishes an article claiming that Christie is a fraud and that his mother is responsible for the writing.

● Write the type of letter you might imagine Christie may write in reply to this article.

Joseph didn't bother to look at the magazine, he just dropped his chin on his chest and listened. Yvonne sallied forward with the written assault on her brother. He listened to the journeyman's doubts, he felt the knife go in between his shoulderblades, he heard the tramp of the jackboots and scholar-like he dwelt on the origin of the writer's name. He smelt burning flesh but his body was ice-cold. "How could he tell such lies?" pondered Nora out loud. "How could he do that to a helpless boy?" asked Matthew. "He shouldn't be let away with it," grumbled Yvonne, but silent Joseph was wondering why the American chose not to mention the poem which he had purposely written in his presence.

Silence reigned when Yvonne threw down the magazine on the floor. She put her arm around her brother's shoulders and hugged him. He didn't bother to react to her concern.

Joseph Meehan the fraud, hinted the cruel big American. Joseph Meehan has a ghost writer, heralded the blundering journeyman. Joseph Meehan never allows folk to see him typing, suggested the cruel-hearted destroyer. Boy that he was, crippled though he was, naive though he was, yet he was old enough in years and wise enough in his soul to know that evil was afoot and determinedly he resolved that he was not going to stumble.

But evil has a way of undermining the bravest. Nora saw her son struggling. She noticed that he seemed weak. She opened wide the back door into the cool green garden. The fresh air blew long lively gusts into his numb mind. Struggling but undefeated, he fought the feelings of rebellion which had now begun to burrow through his soul. Better dead, hinted his rebellious mind, but his mother seemed to sense the screeching in his silence. "Don't heed him, Joseph," advised Nora, "don't heed a coward, he hasn't your guts, don't let him destroy you. Just grit your teeth and see the failure of his article." Then placing her hand under his chin she looked into his hurt eyes and said, "It's too early in your life to have had to confront someone like him."

Matthew was silent for a very long time, then he festered hope in his son by saying, "Listen Joseph, when there's not a word about him people will still be talking about you. So cheer up, don't mind him at all."

The family jollied Joseph along, but when he went to bed that night he cried tears of pristine despair. He sobbed in silence. He was hurt. The hurt of the written assault he might forget, but the fact that a sane man had compared his frantic efforts to speak with the cry of a chastised dog left him hurt beyond freedom, beyond human hope.

Christopher Nolan, *Under the Eye of the Clock*

LISTENING EAR

Listening is a very important yet often much-neglected skill. The Chinese word for listening is made up of all the elements shown here. The way it is constructed suggests that listening is a very active process. How well do you listen?

Options

● With a partner list all the occasions when you listen, categorising each occasion according to the *way* you listen, eg actively, half-heartedly, impatiently, and so on.

● Try the following roleplay exercises to explore just a few ways of listening. Using the maps on *Repromaster 14*, with a partner roleplay the following: A is a stranger to the area and wishes to find out where all the local bed-and-breakfast places are. A is very impatient and a poor listener. B must not show A where to go on the map – he/she must *describe* how to get to the various places. Now swap over: this time B is a stranger to the area and is trying to discover where all the local telephone boxes are as he/she has left something in one, but doesn't know which one. B is a very patient listener. All the other rules apply.

In the same way that you don't have to read every word or sentence or even a whole story to know what's going on, it is also possible to miss the occasional word or more and still make sense of what you're listening to. What has gone before and what follows help you to make (usually) accurate guesses.

● Listen to the tape of a speech. You will notice that several words have been covered up with noise. See how many of these words you can work out. Listen to the speech again, this time listening out for the religious words. List them. Now listen to the speech, this time listening out for the word 'freedom'. Count how many times you hear it.

For many people, the ability to listen is seriously affected. Many people, young and old, suffer from various types of hearing loss. Even the mildest form can seriously affect the way people understand the world about them. Listen to the tape to experience what people with different types of hearing problems have to cope with. To be seriously 'hearing impaired' or to be totally deaf means that you have to rely upon other means of communication. Lip-reading can be a great help. You might try this out. The following rules must be obeyed:
1. *Keep still.*
2. *Look directly towards each other.*
3. *Sit or stand at the same level.*
4. *Talk in a normal voice. Do not shout.*

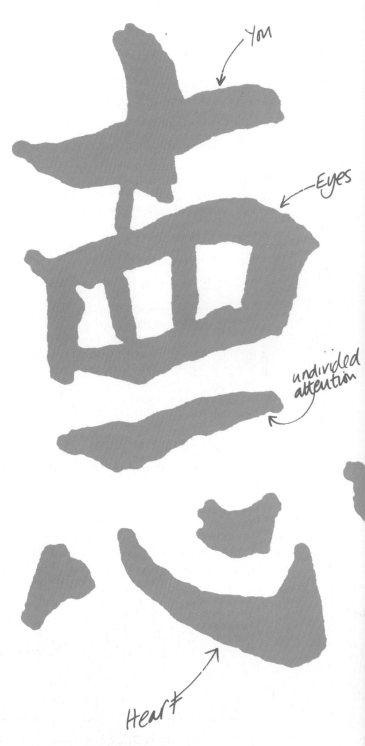

Hearing aids, and radio aids (in school a teacher will wear a microphone around their neck and the child will wear a receiver) can also be helpful but they can't overcome hearing problems in the same way that glasses can overcome sight problems. Sign language for many is the most helpful tool. There are two types in this country: one-handed and, the most common, two-handed:

● Using the examples of 'signs' for whole words (there are hundreds more), together with individual letters for names, etc, have a signed conversation with your partner. Construct a few simple sentences about your family.

Yes Nod the hand as the head
No Shake the hand as the head
Good Thumbs up
Bad Little finger away from self
Sign Palms facing each other and circling
Fingerspell Fingers 'talk' to each other going along
Please Blowing a little kiss
Thank you Blowing two little kisses
Man Beard
Woman Soft cheek, bonnet string
Boy Little or no beard
Girl Little lips
Mother Two Ms
Father Two Fs
Brother Rub knuckles together
Sister Hook finger over nose
Baby Rock one arm on other
Husband Man and ring on finger
Wife Woman and ring on finger

Children Small people
People Man and woman
Old Wrinkles on face
Young Letter Y
You Point to person
I/Me Point to self
Him/Her Point to person
Them Point to people
Us/We Start with self, point to others and end with self
Mine/My 'Belongs' so close fist to self
Yours 'Belongs' so close fist to person
What Index finger up, palm away from body, move finger from side to side
Why 'Y' – place back of hand on opposite shoulder
Who Index finger upright making a circle
Where Palm upwards, circular movement, looking for something
How Upside down W
Because Left hand with thumb up. Tap right fingers on others and then thumb
Have Catch in hand
Can C from nose and chin
Cannot Draw a cross with index finger, turn hand over for last stroke
Nice Thumb across mouth left to right
Beautiful Finger and thumb in circle, other fingers straight, bring O out from mouth
Like Pat chest
Don't like As 'like' and add an outwards, away from body, movement
Love Cross over hands to pat opposite shoulders
Argue Two fingers of both hands curled, move in alternate up and down movement
Fight Both little fingers 'fight' with each other
His/Hers Close fist to person
Theirs Close fist to people
Ours Close fist start with self, round others and end with self
Group Start with thumbs together and shape fingers round to a 'group'
Name N from forehead
Alone/Lonely One finger held up straight motion away from self

Myself As 'Alone' but towards self
Yourself As 'Alone' but to specific person
Themselves As 'Alone' but to the other persons
We As 'Alone', start with self and include other persons
Numbers Tap first knuckles on chin
1 to 5 Number of fingers turning palm out as number is said
6 to 9 Number of fingers added to five on top of other fist
10 Like letter B
11 to 15 Flick fingers up keeping palm towards self
16 to 19 Number of fingers added to 'fifteen' of other hand and coming up from under fist
20, 30, 40, 50 Fingers together making O sign
60, 70, 80, 90 As above but on top of bunched fingers of other hand
Little Finger and thumb a little apart
Small Palms facing bring almost together
Large Opposite to 'small'
Some Stroke thumb across tips
Healthy 'Good' sign with both hands moving up chest
Weak 'Bad' sign moving both hands down chest
Strong Lift arm from elbow to show muscles
Place/Country Pointing arms length
Live/Address Middle finger strokes shoulder on same side
Poor Draw a hole in other elbow
Rich Both hands down front ie rich garments or fur
Here Point here
There Point there
Another Index or middle finger taps end of other middle finger
In Point into space between hand and body
Laugh Finger and thumb make a smile at mouth
House Shape of roof and walls
Car Mime steering wheel
Up Point upwards
Down Point downwards

The Princess of Wales holding a conversation in sign language on a visit to a centre for deaf people.

● See if you can work out your own signs for the following words: crowd, nothing, book, danger, boat, football, expensive, teacher, hungry, cry, god.

Remember: this is not merely a game – for many people this is the main means of communicating with others.

Young people with hearing problems have difficulty with written examinations. Their vocabulary is usually limited because of a lack of use. You might imagine that technical words – vital to the understanding of any subject – would be the hardest to learn, and they are certainly among the most important: imagine trying to learn to read a map if you didn't know what was meant by 'latitude' and 'longitude', 'contour lines' and 'grid references'. But one group of experts says that the most difficult words are those that are called 'carrier' words. Here are some examples, together with the words that the experts suggest they ought to be replaced with:

utilise – use
require – need
adequate – enough
prevent – stop
prior to – before

produce – make
locate – find
current – now
on completion of – when finished
in conjunction with – with

Options

● Look at an examination paper of a subject for which you find the language difficult. Look for difficult 'carrier' words. Draw up a letter to the examination board explaining the difficulties that young people – particularly those with hearing difficulties – can experience with these words, and suggesting alternatives.

● Listen to and discuss the taped examples of how 'hearing impaired' people hear the world.

● Using the guide for teaching hearing impaired children, on *Repromaster 15,* write an open letter to teachers appealing for a greater understanding of the needs and problems of deaf children. Write not only about the things they should take into consideration but also about the things they should do.

● If you listen to the tape, you will hear children with hearing problems talking about the difficulties they encounter. Are there any aspects of their experience that a person with conventional hearing might take for granted?

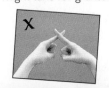

PLEASE UNDERSTAND

There are many people who, for a variety of reasons, cannot express themselves fully in words.

The following piece was written by Wai Keung, a fifteen-year-old schoolboy, newly arrived from Hong Kong, and learning to express himself through the English language.

I put my hands into my two little pockets. I found a photograph. I took it out, it was my grandfather. I lived with him since I was born, but now . . . I have to go away from him and my country. My tears came out. I clean that off quickly with my hands, tried to not let people saw me. I didn't know why I would do that, perhaps because I was new from here.

I kissed the photograph and then put it back inside my pocket carefully because that was the only thing my grandfather had left for me. But perhaps I couldn't say that it was the only thing. I still have my memory.

I saw my parents and my uncle. They took my luggage into the taxis. My father told the taxi driver our address. I felt interesting that my father could talk another kind of language. I thought how could I learn English. It would be hard for me, I thought again. I cried again, but not from my eyes, but from my heart.

Wai Keung

● Listen to the other example, on the tape, of what one person who came to this country some time ago has to say about his experiences.

The second piece was written by John La Rose, a poet from Trinidad living in England, who explains how he cannot bring himself to say what he really feels.

Unsaid

There are things
   one voice
      will never utter
to the four winds of time.

Let my eyes speak
    for me
what my entrails thrill
    to tell
but will not say.

Nothing stops me
    but that me
inside of me that never
    now will see
the light of day.

It is a stranger
    that holds
enthralled in doom
when words could save
    from sheer dismay.

Some day, perhaps, I will tell
    myself why I
should hide from lips
    the things my heart
would say. Some day perhaps.

John La Rose

● With a partner or in a small group, try to identify the most important phrase in each piece. One of the group should report back to the class on the reasons for their choice.

● Take one of these characters and place them in a situation where they have a voice, and write an extended piece of dialogue.

● To get a flavour of what it feels like to express feelings under almost impossible circumstances, write a short paragraph about something you feel strongly about, without using verbs at all. How difficult did you find the exercise? Share your piece with a partner.

● Can you recall a situation when there was something you really wanted to express to someone, but couldn't find the words? Or maybe you can think of someone now, to whom you would like to express something. Write a stream-of-consciousness piece – in other words, write whatever springs to mind, without taking a pause or thinking too hard. (Read it and destroy it if you wish!)

● Improvise a situation where a British tourist is attempting to make him/herself understood in a Spanish restaurant, without a single word of Spanish.

I MEAN TO SAY

The English language is full of oddities – strange phrases that, translated word for word, conjure up bizarre pictures and images. These phrases have become so familiar to us that we hardly give them a second thought – but if you were just beginning to learn English as a second language, what would you make of the following examples?

You tell your Denis to come over this second. His feet aren't to touch the ground. I want to give him a piece of my mind!

Tell your Dad... Nothing doing! I'm putting my foot down!

To be fair and square
To be glad to see the back of someboc
To kill two birds with one stone
To put someone's back up
To be in someone's bad books
To crack up
To give someone a piece of your mind
To flog a dead horse
To name the day
To eat your heart out
To beat about the bush
To give someone the cold shoulder
To put your foot down
To go to pieces
To twist someone round your little fing
To look down in the mouth
To be down in the dumps
To go in one ear and out the other
To let off steam
To eat your own words
To score a bull's eye
To have money to burn
To bite off more than you can chew

Options

● Look at *Repromaster16* for more examples of sayings.

● Write a short piece using as many of these phrases as you can. Then get a friend to translate it word for word. The effect should be quite funny – but you can just imagine the problems which could arise if you were new to the language.

● Try an improvisation based on these phrases. Work with a partner. One of you keeps using some of the phrases; the other interprets them literally. Try holding a conversation.

● Taking one example from the phrases above, write a letter home as a student from overseas explaining the problems the phrase caused you on the occasion when you first heard it.

Now – what can you make of these Jamaican proverbs?

You in de right church but in de wrong pew.
Neber cuss alligator long mout' till you cross riber.
Big ship need deep water.
Cuss cuss break no bones.
New broom sweep clean, but de ole broom knew de carner.
Ebery jackass t'ink him pickney race harse.
Duppy know who fe frighten.
Man nebber know de use a water till de tank dry.
See de candle light befo' you blow out de match.
If you go a tump-a-foot dance, you must dance tump-a-foot.
Hollow gourd mek mos' noise.
Wha' you lose in de jig, you gain in de reel.
Marry fe love, work fe money.
Before you marry keep you two yeye open, after you marry shut one.
No rain, no rainbow.

Anyone unfamiliar with either of the sets of phrases opposite could regard them as secret codes that have to be decoded.

No Rain, No Rainbow

Suppose today
you're feeling down
your face propping a frown

Suppose today
you're one streak of a shadow
the sky giving you a headache

Tomorrow
you never know
you might wake up
in the peak of a glow.

If you don't get the rain
how can you get the rainbow?

Say it again, Granny,
No rain, no rainbow.

Say it again, Granny,
No rain, no rainbow.
John Agard

- Turn an English or Jamaican proverb or a family saying into a poem for small children , explaining the meaning in the process.

You probably know numerous phrases that are like a secret code in your own house. Can you think of any? Are any of these familiar?

Parents' Sayings

You're old enough to wash your own socks.
He's not coming through that door again, I can tell you.
If it's true what your teacher said then you can say
goodbye to that coat we were going to get you.
You do it and like it.
When did you last wash your feet?
Why don't you do a Saturday job?
The answer's NO.
The biscuits are for *everyone* – OK?
Don't mind me, I'm just your mother.
You haven't ridden that bike of yours for years.
You try and leave home and I'll chuck you out on your ear.
You're certainly not going to put that up on any wall in
this house.
Do you know what a Hoover is?
You can pay for the next phone bill.
If you don't like this caff – find another one.
Just 'cos he's doing biology he thinks he's going to be a
brain surgeon.
Do you remember that lovely Christmas when he was six?
Michael Rosen

Options

- What do parents really mean when they use these phrases? Using the storyboard on *Repromaster 17* produce a series of drawings with these phrases (and examples of your own) in 'speech bubbles', and what the people really mean to say in 'thought bubbles'.

- Roleplay the situation of a grandparent examining your new outfit, or your parents listening to a new record you've spent ages saving up for, or you discussing the redecoration of your room that your parents did for you as a surprise. In each situation the characters must be as polite as they can be.

Then try it with four people, the extra two speaking out the true feelings of the two main characters. You could even video this with voice-overs.

On a more serious note, not saying what we really mean or what we really want to say can cause frustration, despair or anger. On the other hand, sometimes it's best not to say what we mean. What do you understand by the word 'assertiveness' or the phrase 'to be outspoken'? What do you understand by the words 'tact' and 'diplomacy'?

- Taking any of the situations listed below, write a piece of dialogue or drama script in which one of the characters is being assertive/outspoken, while the other is being tactful and diplomatic:

a teacher confronting a pupil for bad behaviour;

a customer in a restaurant complaining to the waiter about poor service;

a traffic warden writing out a parking ticket for a motorist who has parked his/her car on double yellow lines.

You might choose, for comic effect, to reverse the roles: in other words, you could make the obviously outspoken character a tactful individual, and vice versa. This might work well as a piece of roleplay, too.

BODY TALK

Body language is something that everyone uses to communicate feelings, attitudes and a whole range of information in addition to what is actually being spoken. A person's posture, facial expressions and various movements of the body can say a lot about what that person is thinking or feeling. Here are just a few examples:

Looking round the room whilst in conversation – boredom/the person is a newcomer/the people know each other very well

Avoiding looking directly at each other – sitting too close for comfort/talking about something painful or difficult to discuss

One person avoiding eye contact – shyness/rudeness/dishonesty/embarrassment/shame/unhappiness

Staring into someone's eyes for long periods during conversation – intention to dominate/threaten

Rapid eye movements – excitement

Eyes 'frozen open' – fear

Looking downwards – sadness

Narrowing of eyes – anger

Raising eyebrows upon meeting someone – greeting

Head held high and slightly backwards – aggression/superiority

Head held low – humility/inferiority/depression

Resting head in palm of hand during conversation – boredom

Propping up head with thumb and two fingers – interest/involvement

Head of speaker tilted to one side – what is being said is not meant to be taken seriously

Frequent nodding of head – continued interest in what the other person is saying

A sudden increase in nodding accompanied by a glance away – desire to end a conversation

Tapping and twitching of feet during conversation – a sign that the person is keeping something to themselves

Moving closer during conversation – the conversation is becoming more private and personal

Folding arms – person is unsympathetic to what is being said

Partners leaning towards each other throughout conversation – mutual affection

Partners leaning away from each other throughout conversation – negative feelings towards each other

Taking a higher position (standing, or on a higher seat) – intention to dominate

Options

● Can you add to the list?

● In a piece of roleplay, create four characters in a group who really exaggerate:
a) a lack of interest
b) friendliness
c) superiority
d) shyness.

Go through the list opposite to select the appropriate body language for your character. Begin your conversation (about, shall we say, your last English lesson, school dinners or homework) with the 'eyebrow flash', a smile, a nod and plenty of eye contact. Add as many of your own ideas as you can. The rest of the class could take notes on the body language you use.

● Watch part of an episode of an English 'soap' together and, either using the list opposite or the checklist on *Repromaster 18*, take note of the types of body language you notice. Are they exaggerated or normal? Do you find characters who use body language more likeable?

Body language can be very different in different societies. Gordon Wainwright gives a few examples:

If you wish to summon a waiter at a business lunch in western countries, a common way is to hold a hand up with the index finger extended. In Asia, however, this is the way you would call a dog or some other animal. In Arab countries, showing the soles of your feet is an insult and an Arab may also insult someone by holding a hand in front of the person's face.

In the United States, you can signal that everything is all right by forming a circle with the thumb and index finger and spreading out the rest of the fingers. But you should remember that in Japan the same gesture means money and in Brazil it is an insult.

We often pat children on the head as a sign of affection, but in Islamic countries the head is regarded as the seat of mental and spiritual powers. Accordingly, it should not be touched.

We scratch our heads when we are puzzled. In Japan, the same action is interpreted as showing anger.

In most parts of the world, shaking the head means 'No', but with Arabs and in parts of Greece, Yugoslavia, Bulgaria and Turkey a more usual way is to toss the head to one side, perhaps clicking the tongue as well. In Japan, a person may move his right hand backwards and forwards to communicate a refusal or disagreement.

On the other hand, agreement is shown in Africa by holding an open palm upright and smacking it with a closed fist. Arabs will show agreement by extending clasped hands with the index fingers pointing towards the other person.

Gordon Wainwright, *Body Language*

Options

● If you get the opportunity to see a foreign film, take note of any unusual forms of body language in it.

● You might like to produce a guide to body language with photographs or drawings. You might even like to produce a short video film. If you choose to do either of these, prepare a storyboard first. (The storyboard blank on *Repromaster 17* might help you.)

● You could try the 'nodding experiment' with members of your family – see if more nodding on your part, midway through a conversation, will increase the amount of talking they do. Does less nodding cause them to clam up?

● There are many specialist uses of particular body signals. You might like to investigate some of these as a class.

ANIMAL TALK

All animals have ways of communicating. Visual symbols are widely used for communication in the animal world, such as the bright colours of birds' plumage used to attract the opposite sex, the vivid patterns on butterflies' wings which are meant for the same purpose and the black and yellow stripes on many flying insects, intended to show potential predators that they are dangerous. Dances are used to both attract and frighten. Bees perform a very complex dance in order to show the other inhabitants of a hive where to find pollen. Some insects even produce their own light, usually to attract mates. (The light of just one cucujo beetle from the West Indies is enough to read by!) Some fishes produce flashes of light to dazzle their pursuers. Some animals produce scents to mark the borders of their territory. The buzz of mosquitoes, the click of crickets, the croaking of frogs, the grunting of pigs, the bleating of sheep, birdsong and so on, all have meaning – provided of course that you are another mosquito, cricket, frog, pig, sheep or bird! The languages used are unknown to us. We can only identify the types of signals.

Options

● Listen to the tape and see if you can decide what messages the animals you are listening to are trying to communicate. (You will find the answers on *Repromaster 19*.)

● Research a particular animal of your choice to discover how it communicates.

● Animals are constantly given voices and personalities in cartoons, in children's books and even in TV advertisements. List all the examples you can think of. How many of the animals portrayed in these ways would be happy with their potrayal? Write a letter as an indignant animal, complaining about the stereotype presented. You might choose to be any one of the numerous cartoon cats who are outwitted by mice or birds, or any one of several cartoon dogs who are portrayed as being stupid or slow.

● Play the drama game around the class where you say, "If 'x' wasn't a person he/she'd be a . . ." Pick the name of an animal that suits their personality. Be careful, though. Avoid the obviously insulting ones: animals like toad and slug don't go down too well! Go round the whole class.

You could then hold an animal rights meeting such as the one that is about to take place in this extract from the beginning of **Animal Farm***:*

Mr Jones, of the Manor Farm, had locked the hen-houses for the night, but was too drunk to remember to shut the pop-holes. With the ring of light from his lantern dancing from side to side he lurched across the yard, kicked off his boots at the back door, drew himself a last glass of beer from the barrel in the scullery, and made his way up to bed, where Mrs Jones was already snoring.

As soon as the light in the bedroom went out there was a stirring and a fluttering all through the farm buildings. Word had gone round during the day that old Major, the prize Middle White boar, had had a strange dream on the previous night and wished to communicate it to the other animals. It had been agreed that they should all meet in the big barn as soon as Mr Jones was safely out of the way. Old Major (so he was always called, though the name under which he had been exhibited was Willingdon Beauty) was so highly regarded on the farm that everyone was quite ready to lose an hour's sleep in order to hear what he had to say.

At one end of the big barn, on a sort of raised platform, Major was already ensconced on his bed of straw, under a lantern which hung from a beam. He was twelve years old and had lately grown rather stout, but he was still a majestic-looking pig, with a wise and benevolent appearance in spite of the fact that his tushes had never been cut. Before long the other animals began to arrive and make themselves comfortable after their different fashions. First came the three dogs, Bluebell, Jessie and Pincher, and then the pigs, who settled down in the straw immediately in front of the platform. The hens perched themselves on the window-sills, the pigeons fluttered up to the rafters, the sheep and cows lay down behind the pigs and began to chew the cud. The two cart-horses, Boxer and Clover, came in together, walking very slowly and setting down their vast hairy hoofs with great care lest there should be some small animal concealed in the straw. Clover was a stout motherly mare approaching middle life, who had never quite got her figure back after her fourth foal. Boxer was an enormous beast, nearly eighteen hands high, and as strong as any two ordinary horses put together. A white stripe down his nose gave him a somewhat stupid appearance, and in fact he was not of first-rate intelligence, but he was universally respected for his steadiness of character and tremendous powers of work. After the horses came Muriel, the white goat, and Benjamin the donkey. Benjamin was the oldest animal on the farm, and the worst tempered. He seldom talked, and when he did it was usually to make some cynical remark – for instance he would say that God had given him a tail to keep the flies off, but that he would sooner have had no tail and no flies. Alone among the animals on the farm he never laughed. If asked why, he would say that he saw nothing to laugh at. Nevertheless, without openly admitting it, he was devoted to Boxer; the two of them usually spent their Sundays together in the small paddock beyond the orchard, grazing side by side and never speaking.

The two horses had just lain down when a brood of ducklings which had lost their mother filed into the barn, cheeping feebly and wandering from side to side to find some place where they would not be trodden on. Clover made a sort of wall round them with her great foreleg, and the ducklings nestled down inside it and promptly fell asleep. At the last moment Mollie, the foolish, pretty white mare who drew Mr Jones's trap, came mincing daintily in, chewing at a lump of sugar. She took a place near the front and began flirting her white mane, hoping to draw attention to the red ribbons it was plaited with. Last of all came the cat, who looked round, as usual, for the warmest place, and finally squeezed herself in between Boxer and Clover; there she purred contentedly throughout Major's speech without listening to a word of what he was saying.

All the animals were now present except Moses, the tame raven, who slept on a perch behind the back door. When Major saw that they had all made themselves comfortable and were waiting attentively he cleared his throat and began:

"Comrades, you have heard already about the strange dream that I had last night. But I will come to the dream later. I have something else to say first. I do not think, comrades, that I shall be with you for many months longer, and before I die I feel it my duty to pass on to you such wisdom as I have acquired. I have had a long life, I have had much time for thought as I lay alone in my stall, and I think I may say that I understand the nature of life on this earth as well as any animal now living. It is about this that I wish to speak to you.

"Now, comrades, what is the nature of this life of ours? Let us face it, our lives are miserable, laborious and short. We are born, we are given just so much food as will keep the breath in our bodies, and those of us who are capable of it are forced to work to the last atom of our strength; and the very instant that our usefulness has come to an end we are slaughtered with hideous cruelty. No animal in England knows the meaning of happiness or leisure after he is a year old. No animal in England is free. The life of an animal is misery and slavery: that is the plain truth."
George Orwell, *Animal Farm*

George Orwell gave his animals a voice in order to make political points about the nature of revolution and tyranny; but with numerous species now facing extinction, many conservationists and writers attempt to give the animals a voice with which to beg for mercy.

● Research into any endangered species, and produce an open letter to the human race supposedly from the animal in question, giving details of feeding habits, habitat, etc., and showing how hunting and environmental problems are threatening your survival. The point of your letter is to make people aware of the plight of an endangered species. To do that you need to supply a lot of factual information to back up your appeal for mercy. Your plan for such a letter should include a list of the facts you wish to communicate and the points you wish to get across that you hope will arouse sympathy in your readers. Endangered species include the Giant Panda, the Mountain Gorilla, the Polar Bear, the Orangutan, and hundreds more.

Killing a Whale

A whale is killed as follows:
A shell is filled with dynamite and
A harpoon takes the shell.
You wait until the great grey back
Breaches the sliding seas, you squint,
Take aim.
The cable snakes like a squirt of paint,
The shell channels deep through fluke
And flank, through mural softness
To bang among the blubber,
Exploding terror through
The hollow fleshy chambers,
While the hooks fly open
Like an umbrella
Gripping the tender tissue.

It dies with some panache,
Whipping the capstan like
A schoolboy's wooden top,
Until the teeth of the machine
Can hold its anger, grip.
Its dead tons thresh for hours
The ravished sea,
Then sink together, sag –
So air is pumped inside
To keep the corpse afloat,
And one of those flags that men
Kill mountains with is stuck
Into this massive death.

Dead whales are rendered down,
Give oil.

David Gill

Options

● Research the particular plight of whales, and, armed with such information, produce a 'letter from a whale', to be used as a piece of publicity material with the intention of stirring the reader into action, encouraging protest against our inhumanity towards these creatures.

LANGUAGE COMMUNITY

In every community we can find a rich and unique variety of language on display. It appears in local dialects, in curious street names, and in signs and shopfronts using languages other than English, and it's this diversity that gives local community language its rich, distinct flavour.

Explore the variety of language to be found in the community, using the ideas below simply as starting points.

Options

● How many different influences/languages can you find in your town?

● Can you find any examples of local dialect on display?

● Make a guidebook or video or photopack with written commentary about the languages, old and new, in your local community.

● Using a world map as a central display, you could indicate with arrows the origins of local influences/languages.

GIVING THE COMMUNITY A VOICE

● Search for graffiti that expresses opinions in your area on subjects such as sexism, housing, unemployment, etc. Look for letters to your local paper from members of the community, on local issues.

Discover if there are any petitions currently being circulated. Are there any pressure groups concerned with housing or environment issues? Have there been any factory closures? Has there been any new building?

Or try asking elderly people for their views on young people today – or local women from a variety of professions (how about bus-drivers, policewomen, dinner ladies, teachers) on the role of women today.

First, within the class, identify sympathisers and opponents to the views expressed, then prepare questions to ask within the local community. Remember – your aim is to encourage people to talk freely, rather than simply give a long list of short answers to a long list of questions.

You might choose to present your work as a special issue of a local newspaper containing a variety of articles on the subject, together with photos, sketches, letters, and so on.

VARIATIONS

Morning Song

Love set you going like a fat gold watch.
The midwife slapped your footsoles, and your bald cry
Took its place among the elements.

Our voices echo, magnifying your arrival. New statue
In a drafty museum, your nakedness
Shadows our safety. We stand round blankly as walls.

I'm no more your mother
Than the cloud that distils a mirror to reflect its own slow
Effacement at the wind's hand.

All night your moth-breath
Flickers among the flat pink roses. I wake to listen:
A far sea moves in my ear.

One cry, and I stumble from bed, cow-heavy and floral
In my Victorian nightgown.
Your mouth opens clean as a cat's. The window square

Whitens and swallows its dull stars. And now you try
Your handful of notes:
The clear vowels rise like balloons.
Sylvia Plath

Slow Reader

He can make sculptures
And fabulous machines
Invent games, tell jokes
Give solemn, adult advice
But he is slow to read.
When I take him on my knee
With his *Ladybird* book
He gazes into the air
Sighing and shaking his head
Like an old man
Who knows the mountains
Are impassable.

He toys with words
Letting them grow cold
As gristly meat
Until I relent
And let him wriggle free –
A fish returning
To its element
Or a white-eyed colt
Shying from the bit
As if he sees
That if he takes it
In his mouth
He'll never run
Quite free again.

Vicki Feaver

Who can speak of your living
Describe your beauty and grace,
Explain that you are crying
When there's laughter on your face.

You have the words and wisdom,
The power in your soul.
Tell the poem, write the story
Let the words unfold.
Su Andi

Poem for a Dead Poet

He was a poet he was.
A proper poet.
He said things
that made you think
and said them nicely.
He saw things
that you or I
could never see
and saw them clearly.
He had a way
with language.
Images flocked around
him like birds,
St Francis, he was,
of the words. Words?
Why he could almost make 'em talk.

Roger McGough

STRUCTURES

A HISTORY OF THE ENGLISH LANGUAGE

The English language 'arrived' in this country in the fifth century AD, with invading tribes of Angles, Saxons and Jutes. Before the arrival of these peoples, England had been inhabited for at least 50,000 years, possibly even as much as 250,000 years.

Our earliest knowledge of a language spoken in Britain is of that spoken by the Celts who arrived from about 500 BC onwards. The Celtic language is still represented in Irish and Scots Gaelic, and in Welsh.

● Listen to the extracts on tape.

Ba mhinic do shíl Nóra go mba bhreá an saol bheith ag imeacht roimpi ina seabhac siúil gan beann aici ar dhuine ar bith – bóithre na hÉireann roimpi agus a haghaidh orthu; cúl a cinn leis an mbaile agus le cruatan agus le crostacht a muintire; í ag siúl ó bhaile go baile agus ó ghleann go gleann. An bóthar breá réidh roimpi, glasra ar gach taobh de, tithe beaga cluthara ar shleasa na gcnocán.

Several times before Nora had thought of what a fine life she would have as a tramp, independent of everybody! Her face on the roads of Ireland before her, and her back on home and the hardship and anger of her family! To walk from village to village and from glen to glen, the fine level road before her, with green fields on both sides of her and small well-sheltered houses on the mountain slopes around her!

Padraic Pearse, *The Roads*

Pam y caiff bwystfilod rheibus
   Dorri'r egin mân i lawr?
Pam caiff blodau peraid ifainc
   Fethu gan y sychdwr mawr?
Dere â'r cafodydd hyfryd
   Sy'n cynyddu'r egin grawn,
Cafod hyfryd yn y bore
   Ac un arall y prynhawn.

Why are ravenous beasts allowed
   To trample the tender grapes?
Why must sweet flowers
   Fail in the great drought?
Send the healing showers
   To increase the vine shoots,
A healing shower of the first rain
   And another of the latter rain.

William Williams Pantycelyn

In 55 BC Julius Caesar and his Roman army invaded England, but with only limited success, and it was not until the year 43 AD that a comprehensive conquest of England by the Emperor Claudius and his army took place. The Romans remained in power in England for over three hundred years. However, Latin, the language of the conquerors, was not very widely spoken during this time. Its use was confined mainly to the inhabitants of cities and to members of the upper classes. It certainly didn't replace the Celtic language, nor did it survive the invasion in 449 AD by the Teutonic tribes (Angles, Saxons and Jutes).

● Listen to the extract on tape.

Quae potest homini esse polito delectatio, cum aut homo imbecillus a valentissima bestia laniatur aut praeclara bestia venabulo transverberatur? quae tamen, si videnda sunt, saepe vidisti; neque nos, qui haec spectamus, quicquam novi vidimus. Extremus elephantorum dies fuit. In quo admiratio magna vulgi atque turbae, delectatio nulla exstitit; quin etiam misericordia quaedam consecuta est atque opinio est modi, esse quamdam illi beluae cum genere humano societatem.

What sort of kick can a civilized person get out of watching some poor beggar being torn to bits by a hulking great animal, or, for that matter, a beautiful animal being shot through with a hunting spear? Even if these things were worth seeing, you've seen them often enough, and those of us watching saw nothing new. The last day was elephant day; and for all the enthusiasm of the crowd, there was no fun in it; we were left more with a feeling of pity, and the sense that there is a certain kinship between that huge animal and the human race.

Cicero

From this time a long succession of invaders from Denmark and neighbouring lands conquered more and more of England. The Jutes settled largely in Kent, while the Angles settled on the East coast, north of the Humber, and in East Anglia. The Saxons occupied the areas known today as Essex and Middlesex (kingdoms of the East Saxons and Middle Saxons). The Celts were largely driven to Cornwall and Wales, and Roman towns were destroyed. Some Celts, however, did remain where they were.

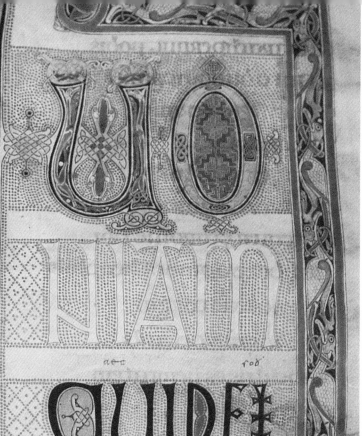

The Angles and Saxons combined forces to form several kingdoms: Mercia, East Anglia, Kent, Essex, Wessex and Northumbria. The differences in language between the three tribes were very slight. The English language of today is formed largely of the dialects spoken by the Angles, Saxons and Jutes. In its earliest form it is known as Old English.

Wessex was the most important area of England at that time, and because of this, most surviving records come from that region. As a result, we know more about the West Saxon dialect than any other.

● Listen to the extract on tape.

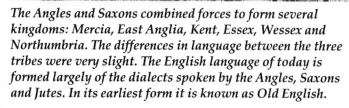

Beowulf maþelode,   bearn Ecgþeowes:
"Ne sorga, snotor guma!   Selre bið æghwæm
þæt he his freond wrece,   þonne he fela murne.
Ure æghwylc sceal   ende gebidan
worolde lifes;   wyrce se þe mote
domes ær deaþe;   þæt bið drihtguman
unlifgendum   æfter selest.
Aris, rices weard;   uton hraþe feran
Grendles magan   gang sceawigan.
Ic hit þe gehate: no he on helm losaþ,
ne on foldan fæþm,   ne on fyrgenholt,
ne on gyfenes grund,   ga þær he wille.
Ðys dogor þu   geþyld hafa
weana gehwylces,   swa ic þe wene to."

Beowulf spoke, the son of Ecgtheow: "Do not be sorrowful, wise man! It is better for anyone that he should avenge his friend, rather than mourn greatly. Each of us must await the end of life in this world; let him who can, achieve glory before death; afterwards, when lifeless, that will be best for a noble man. Rise up, guardian of the kingdom; let us go swiftly to examine the trail of Grendel's relative. I promise you this: she will not escape under cover, neither in the bosom of the earth, nor in the mountain forest, nor at the bottom of the ocean, go where she will. For today, have patience in every affliction, as I expect you to."

Beowulf

Old English requires special study to understand it – it is so unfamiliar to us in spelling, pronunciation, vocabulary and grammar. Below are some examples:

hlud = loud   hlaf = load
halig = holy   heafod = head

Old English contained no borrowed words from French, a major influence on Middle and modern-day English. It was, however, slightly influenced by the Celts. Celtic names for places, in particular, remain with us today. The river Thames and the river Avon are two examples (Avon comes from the Celtic word for 'river'). Old English was also influenced by Latin: the three tribes brought many Latin words with them due to their contact with the Romans prior to the invasion. In addition, they adopted Latin words being used by the Celts, and they continued to borrow words from the Romans. Many of these words had religious connections – for example prophet, apostle, and demon (words which the Romans had in turn borrowed from the Greeks) – and were first introduced with the coming of Christianity to the Anglo-Saxons in 597.

The third major influence on Old English came from the Vikings of Scandinavia as a result of their frequent attacks and numerous settlements in England between the middle of the eighth century and up to their final conquest of England at the beginning of the eleventh century.

Over 1,400 places in England have Scandinavian names – an indication of the extent to which the Vikings influenced the language. (Look for town names ending in 'by', 'thwaite' and 'toft', as well as those containing the word 'thorp'.) Other words that can be traced from the Viking age are largely to do with everyday life, eg birth, bull, calf, dirt, egg, fellow, kid, leg, loan, race, root, sister, sky and so on. A large number of words were adopted into the language as the Anglo-Saxon and Viking races merged, between the tenth and eleventh centuries.

The Norman conquest in 1066 changed the whole face of the English language. For the next two hundred years the language of the upper classes was French, while the mass of the population continued to speak English. The historian known as Robert of Gloucester described the situation in 1300.

● Listen to the extract on tape

þus com lo engelond in to normandies hond.
& þe normans ne couþe speke þo bote hor owe speche
& speke french as hii dude atom, & hor children dude also teche
So þat heiemen of þis lond þat of hor blod come
Holdeþ alle þulke speche þat hii of hom nome.

Vor bote a man conne frenss me telþ of him lute
Ac lowe men holdeþ to engliss & to hor owe speche ȝute.
Ich wene þer ne beþ in al þe world contreyes none
þat ne holdeþ to hor owe speche bote engelond one.
Ac wel me wot uor to conne boþe wel it is,
Vor þe more þat a mon can, þe more wurþe he is.

Lo! Thus came England into Normandy's control
And the Normans knew only how to speak their own
    language then
And spoke French as they did at home, and also taught
    their children;
So that nobles of this land that came of their blood
Maintain that same speech that they took from them.

For unless a man knows French men think of him little.
But low men hold to English and to their own speech yet.
I think that in all the world there are no countries
That do not keep to their own language except England
    alone.
But men well know that it is good to know both,
For the more that a man knows, the more he is worth.

Robert of Gloucester

By the year 1200 a considerable number of people in England were bilingual as French worked its way down into the 'middle classes'. But by the fourteenth century, English had become once more the language of all English people, and French almost totally disappeared. The Hundred Years war with France (1337–1454) was a powerful influence in the reintroduction of English as a 'national language' on all levels of society.

The influence of the previous two hundred years' use of French resulted in the introduction of over ten thousand French words into the English language. Over three quarters of these are still in use today, eg: adventure, age, air, business, city, fact, joy, reason, rage, spirit and so on.

The period between 1150 and 1500 is known as the 'Middle English' period. The language spoken in England by the end of this period is easily identifiable as a language very close to the one we use today.

● Listen to the extract on tape.

Bifel that in that seson on a day,
In Southwerk at the Tabard as I lay
Redy to wenden on my pilgrimage
To Caunterbury with ful devout corage,
At night was come into that hostelrye
Wel nyne and twenty in a companye
Of sondry folk, by aventure y-falle
In felawshipe, and pilgrims were they alle,
That toward Caunterbury wolden ryde.
The chambres and the stables weren wyde,
And wel we weren esed atte beste.
And shortly, whan the sonne was to reste,
So hadde I spoken with hem everichon,
That I was of hir felawshipe anon,
And made forward erly for to ryse,
To take our wey, ther as I yow devyse.

It befell that one day in that season,
as I was in Southwark at the Tabard Inn,
ready to go on my pilgrimage
to Canterbury with a most devout heart,
at night there came into that hostelry
a company of nine-and-twenty people –
all sorts of people, who had met by chance;
and all of them were pilgrims
who were riding toward Canterbury.
The chambers and the stables were spacious,
and we were made most comfortable.
And shortly, when the sun had gone down,
I had spoken with every one of them
so that I had soon become one of their group,
and made an arrangement to rise early
to be on our way, as I shall tell you.

Chaucer, *The Canterbury Tales*

Borrowing from Latin also continued during this time, particularly words which had connections with law, science, the church and literature, eg *conspiracy, custody, homicide, pulpit, scripture, testimony* and so on.

One of the most notable features of 'Middle English' was the very distinct differences in dialects. The map below shows the rough boundaries together with a simple example (third person singular of the verb 'to love').

Third person singular of the verb 'to love':

loves

loven

loveth

As you will see later in this book, during the fifteenth century a 'standard English' emerged. William Caxton introduced the printing press to Britain in 1476. The development of printing meant that a uniform language, based on the English dialect spoken in London at the time, was being widely communicated throughout England. This did not mean the end of other dialects, however, nor did it mean the end of any further influences on the language. During the sixteenth and seventeenth centuries, the exploration of other lands and the beginning of international commerce resulted in the introduction of many words from Italian and Spanish together with more Greek, Latin and French.

In the eighteenth century the language continued to be standardised and 'tidied up'. 1755 saw the publication of the first dictionary, **A Dictionary of the English Language**, by Samuel Johnson.

Johnson wrote:

"This is my idea of an English dictionary by which the pronunciation of our language may be fixed, and its attainment facilitated; by which its purity may be preserved, its use ascertained, and its duration lengthened."

During the nineteenth century, due to Britain's involvement with many countries around the world, the language gained hundreds of words from North America, the West Indies, India, Africa and Australia. The great developments in science and in every area of intellectual activity, greater interest in sport and leisure, and giant steps forward in industry all combined to extend the vocabulary of the English language. In the twentieth century the developments in technology, the influence of newspapers, the continued borrowing from other languages, even the two world wars, continued to extend what was already the largest vocabulary of any language in the world.

At the present time English is spoken by over 260 million people throughout the world, one tenth of the world's population. Only Chinese is spoken by more people.

William Caxton presenting the Duchess of Burgundy with a copy of his *Recuyell of Historyes Troye*.

ROOTS OF LANGUAGE

If you cannot understand my argument, and declare "It's Greek to me", you are quoting Shakespeare; if you claim to be more sinned against than sinning, you are quoting Shakespeare; if you recall your salad days, you are quoting Shakespeare; if you act more in sorrow than in anger, if your wish is father to the thought, if your lost property has vanished into thin air, you are quoting Shakespeare; if you have ever refused to budge an inch or suffered from green-eyed jealousy, if you have played fast and loose, if you have been tongue-tied, a tower of strength, hoodwinked or in a pickle, if you have knitted your brows, made a virtue of necessity, insisted on fair play, slept not one wink, stood on ceremony, danced attendance (on your lord and master), laughed yourself into stitches, had short shrift, cold comfort or too much of a good thing, if you have seen better days or lived in a fool's paradise – why, be that as it may, the more fool you, for it is a foregone conclusion that you are (as good luck would have it) quoting Shakespeare; if you think it is early days and clear out bag and baggage, if you think it is high time and that that is the long and short of it, if you believe that the game is up and that truth will out even if it involves your own flesh and blood, if you lie low till the crack of doom because you suspect foul play, if you have your teeth set on edge (at one fell swoop) without rhyme or reason, then – to give the devil his due – if the truth were known (for surely you have a tongue in your head) you are quoting Shakespeare; even if you bid me good riddance and send me packing, if you wish I was dead as a door-nail, if you think I am an eyesore, a laughing stock, the devil incarnate, a stony-hearted villain, bloody-minded or a blinking idiot, then – by Jove! O Lord! Tut, tut! for goodness' sake! what the dickens! but me no buts – it is all one to me, for you are quoting Shakespeare.

Bernard Levin, *Enthusiasms*

An original story in which **every word has an Old English** *background:*

At the stroke of five each morning Mother and Father leaped out of bed. Then they began to do many chores about the house. Before the sun rose Mother took water from the well while Father went out into the fields to feed the cows and look after the horses. In summer or in winter, in good weather or bad, everything had to be cared for.

As a small child I often thought how much they must have hated that daily work. Yet they never showed anything but love and hope in our home. They bore hardship without one word of sorrow, and even found time to teach the children how to swim and ride horseback. In the evenings, at dusk, they also taught us the Gospel and little songs about the goodness of God and the wonderful gift of life. They were so thankful that they could give us food to eat and milk to drink as we grew up. They were kind and loving indeed! To my brother and sister and me they were not only kinfolk but true friends.

Modern English	Middle English	Old English
at	at, atte	æt
the	the	thĕ
stroke	stroke, strake	strican
of	of	of
five	fif	fif
each	ech, elc	ælc, æghwile
morning	morweninge	morgen
mother	moder	modor
and	and, an	and, ond
father	fader	faeder
leap	lepen	hleapan
out	out	ūt
bed	bed	bedd

This is not as easy as it may seem.

Options

● Write a few sentences about what you did at the weekend. With the help of a good dictionary explore how many of your words are Old English in origin.

● Using a good dictionary produce your own root and branch picture of words based on original Latin roots such as "spec/spect".

● To investigate the close relationships between languages further, listen to the extracts from a wide variety of languages on the cassette. At the same time, explore the transcriptions on *Repromaster 21*. Search for similarities between the languages you see and hear.

● Produce a Child's Guide to the English Language' using the information supplied on the last few pages, together with anything you can discover from your own research. (The time-chart on *Repromaster 22* should also be useful.) Your intended audience might be a first year English class. The end result should be a pamphlet that is informative and fun.

Use a layout similar to this page.

Include a time-chart, games and activities. Think very hard about what type of presentation might interest an eleven-year-old: use puzzles, quizzes and cartoons, for example, to get facts across. Then try it out.

SPELLING

If you have ever worried about your ability to spell, or felt ashamed or annoyed at the number of corrections in bright red ink on your work, you are not alone.

● Listen to the adults on the tape discussing the difficulties they have had with spelling.

English spelling has been called 'chaotic', and there is no doubt that English is a highly complicated language to spell. The number of ways of spelling the same sound, for example, can go into double figures.

There are at least twelve spellings for 'sh': shoe, sugar, mansion, mission, nation, suspicion, ocean, conscious, chaperon, schedule, fuchsia and pshaw.

Consider the wide variety of endings of words in the plural:

Why English is so Hard

We'll begin with a box, and the plural is boxes;
But the plural of ox should be oxen, not oxes.
Then one fowl is goose, but two are called geese;
Yet the plural of moose should never be meese.
You may find a lone mouse or a whole lot of mice,
But the plural of house is houses, not hice.
If the plural of man is always called men,
Why shouldn't the plural of pan be called pen?
The cow in the plural may be cows or kine.
But the plural of vow is vows, not vine.
And I speak of a foot, and you show me your feet,
But I give you a boot – would a pair be called beet?
If one is a tooth and a whole set are teeth,
Why shouldn't the plural of booth be called beeth?
If the singular is this, and the plural is these,
Should the plural of kiss be nicknamed kese?
Then one may be that, and three may be those,
Yet the plural of hat would never be hose.
We speak of a brother, and also of brethren,
But though we say mother, we never say methren.
The masculine pronouns are he, his and him,
But imagine the feminine she, shis, and shim!
So our English, I think you will all agree,
Is the trickiest language you ever did see.
Anon

It is no surprise that many feel totally frustrated at their inability to spell!

Options

● Investigate problem words and common errors made by your friends or your family. You might try and help them overcome the problems by getting them to write the word repeatedly, cover it, then write it again.

● Interview people in the community about their ability to spell and write up a report on your findings.

● Investigate common errors in written work done by first years in your school. (You might even set them a piece of work which you can mark.) Then, in pairs, devise a card game or board game that might help them overcome a problem by teaching them one spelling rule. For example, they might be required to identify a correct spelling before they move around a board, and they might choose harder words to spell if they want to move around the board faster. Players may have the choice of 'ie' or 'ei' to fill in a gap in words on the board, or double 'l' or single 'l' to complete a word. 'Chance' cards may contain tricky words to be spelt, and so on.

● Produce a radio quiz programme in which teams have to spell difficult words, spell words backwards, give examples of five words with 'ie' in them or ending in 'ission' within a certain time limit, and so on.

The development of English spelling may help to explain why it is so chaotic. Look at the following piece of Old English, and listen to the recording on the tape. Quite difficult to recognise as English, isn't it? But this was the language spoken and written between 450 and 1150 in England.

Fæder ūre,
þū þe eart on heofonum,
sī þīn nama gehālgod.
Tōbecume þīn rīce.
Gewurþe ðīn willa on eorðan swā swā on heofonum.
Ūrne gedæghwāmlīcan hlāf syle ūs tō dæg.
And forgyf ūs ūre gyltas, swā swā wē forgyfað ūrum gyltendum.
And ne gelǣd þū ūs on costnunge,
ac ālȳs ūs of yfele. Sōþlīce.

The most striking thing about Old English is undoubtedly the differences in spelling. Many words were pronounced then as they are today. French and Latin influences dramatically transformed the English language into what is called Middle English (1150–1500). Hundreds and hundreds of words came from the French, such as government, crown, royal, court, subject, traitor, liberty, public, governor, lord, lady, prince, slave, religion, lesson, saint, mercy. The list is almost endless. Similarly from Latin we took a huge number of words, such as incredible, inferior, necessary, picture, polite, private, script, prosecute, pulpit and reject. At this time the way things

were written down was fairly close to the way they were pronounced, but there were many exceptions. The fact that Middle English was formed from several languages and that there were so many dialects around the country gave William Caxton, the man who introduced printing into this country, a considerable headache.

Certaynly it is harde to playse every man by cause of dyversite & chaunge of langage. For in these days every man that is in ony reputacyon in his countre, wyll utter his commynycacyon and maters in suche maners & termes that fewe men shall understonde theym . . .

   I have reduced & translated this sayd booke in to our englysshe, not ouer rude ne curyous, but in suche termes as shall be understanden, by goddys grace, accordynge to my copye.
William Caxton

Incidentally, he 'fixed' the language on the printed page as he heard it used in London, before there was a nationwide agreement on spelling and pronunciation. This was a major cause of the chaos in our spelling. Many have urged simplification and clarification since Caxton's time. Richard Mulcaster, for example, had this to say in 1582:

It were a thing verie praiseworthie in my opinion, and no lesse profitable then praise worthie, if som one well learned and as laborious a man, wold gather all the words which we vse in our English tung, whether naturall or incorporate, out of all professions, as well learned as not, into one dictionarie, and besides the right writing, which is incident to the Alphabete, wold open vnto vs therein, both their naturall force, and their proper vse: that by his honest trauell we might be as able to iudge of our own tung, which we haue by rote, as we ar of others, which we learn by rule. The want whereof, is the onelie cause why, that varie manie men, being excellentlie well learned in foren speche, can hardlie discern what theie haue at home.
Richard Mulcaster, *Elementarie*, 1582

In the early eighteen hundreds, Noah Webster, who later produced several dictionaries himself, expressed his feelings about spelling as follows. (The first list of words that he refers to are Middle English words whose spelling was changed in the sixteenth century.)

In the essays, ritten within the last yeer, a considerable change of spelling iz introduced by way of experiment. This liberty waz taken by the writers before the age of queen Elizabeth, and to this we are indeted for the preference of modern spelling over that of Gower and Chaucer. The man who admits that the change of *housbonde, mynde, ygone, moneth* into *husband, mind, gone, munth*, iz an improovment, must acknowlege also the riting of *helth, breth, rong, tung, month*, to be an improovment. There iz no alternativ. Every possible reezon that could ever be offered for altering the spelling of wurds, stil exists in full force; and if a gradual reform should not be made in our language, it will proov that we are less under the influence of reezon than our ancestors.
Noah Webster

Webster's ideas can be seen today in American spellings such as color, favorite, and so on. In more recent times serious attempts have been made to persuade us to change our spelling. One of the most famous was a book produced in 1908, called **Nue Spelling,** *from which the following was taken:*

Gon Out

A man went too hiz naiborz hous and rang the bel. The maidservant oepnd the dor. "I wish too speek too eur maaster," hee sed. "Hee'z gon out," shee aanserd. "Then I wil speek too eur mis-tris ," hee sed. "Shee'z gon out, too." "That's a piti; but per-haps thai'l soon kum bak. I wil kum in and sit by the fyer and wait for them." "I'm sori, ser," the maid sed, "but the fyer'z gon out too."

Options

● How important is it to spell correctly? What do you think about 'simplified spelling'?

● You could try an experiment in simplification yourself: take a nursery rhyme and rewrite it in 'Nue Spelling'.

● Write a letter in 'Nue Spelling' to a newspaper, recommending its use.

● Listen to the examples of Old English and Middle English on the cassette and follow the transcript on *Repromaster 23*. Underline the words that are familiar. Using a good dictionary, you might like to find the origins of the words in the Middle English piece.

● Write a letter to the Advertising Standards Authority complaining about the use of misspelt words (eg *Weetabix*, *Rice Krispies* – collect as many as you can) exploring the point of view that it sets a bad example for children.

THEM'S THE RULES

Learning the Rules

1. Don't use no double negatives.
2. Always take care with apostrophe's.
3. Always make sure you check through your work just to make sure you haven't any words out.
4. Take grate care with your spelling.
5. And try not to start your sentences with the word 'and'.
6. Don't forget to use a full stop. at the end of a sentence

The following completely disregards any type of rule. Does it still make sense?

According to My Mood

I have poetic licence, i WriTe thE way i waNt.
i drop my full stops where i like . . .
MY CAPITAL LeteRs go where i liKE.
i order from MY PeN, i verse the way i like (i do my
    spelling write)
Acording to My MOod.
i HAve poetic licence,
i put my commers where i like,,((( )).
(((my brackets are write((
I REPEAT WHen i likE
i can't go rong,
i look and i.c.
It's rite.
i REpeat when i liKe. i have
poetic licence!
don't question me????

Benjamin Zephaniah

Making fun of rules, or even deliberately destroying the rules as we see in the poem above, may be enjoyable, but consider the problem created by the lack of punctuation in the sentences below:

The teacher said the child is stupid
The teacher said the child is stupid

If, however, you were to write a couple of sentences to go before the one used above, the meaning of the sentence would be very clear. Try it.

Punctuation, then, is most useful when the meaning of the sentence isn't absolutely clear.

The system of signs and symbols that makes the printed word more easily understood has been in existence almost as long as writing itself. The first example to be discovered dates back to 850 BC.

The rather unusual point about punctuation in the English language, however, is that some of it comes rather late in the sentence to be really helpful. In Spain, for example, a question mark is to be found at the beginning and at the end of a question.

¿Cómo pasas tus ratos libres en casa?

How do you spend your spare time at home?

The same applies to exclamation marks.
In French, any sentence containing direct speech is marked as follows:

« Quel jour était-ce? demandai-je, tirant mon carnet pour prendre consciencieusement note.

– 29 février, dit Adrien. Fallait une année bissextile pour un truc comme ça! »

"What day was that?" I asked, taking out my notebook in order to make notes conscientiously.

"29th of February," said Adrien. "It had to be a leap-year for a thing like that!"

● To help you understand how punctuation makes the meaning of the written word clearer, try the following exercise. With a partner write a short piece of conversation without punctuation. Now give one copy of what you have written to another pair. Read from your copy, taking great care to show what is actually being spoken (to help them put in speech marks on their copy), to show when you are taking a rest (to help them put commas on their copy), and so on. Make your piece of writing as difficult as you can so that it is a real challenge. How close can the other pair get to your original, punctuated version?

You might be forgiven for thinking that the rules of punctuation aren't totally clear. For example, is 'Mrs.' a sentence? Why not? It starts with a capital letter and ends with a full stop.

Options

● Have fun with the rules. Create your own set of rules like those at the top of the previous page.

● Write a short piece in which you deliberately destroy the rules, as in the poem by Benjamin Zephaniah.

● You might invent your own punctuation system based on road signs, traffic lights or anything else you care to use.

● In a group of five or six, plan an advertising campaign to 'sell' a punctuation mark to younger pupils – you could produce posters, leaflets, jingles, storyboards for advertisements, simple animations (using overhead projector transparencies), or you might like to make handpuppets for videoing advertisements. Run your campaign as a real advertising agency would, with planning meetings to discuss, select and reject ideas and to decide who does what.

● In a group, produce a handbook of punctuation tips and exercises for first years. You will need to discuss the needs of eleven-year-olds first. Make it lively and interesting. You might include cartoon characters, comic strips, puzzles, and exercises where pupils have to fill in the punctuation.

Though the following extract was written in 1466, it is true that many people are still unclear on the exact rules concerning several punctuation marks. (Try asking all your teachers when a semi-colon should be used, for example.)

● Rewrite the extract below in a simplified and more up-to-date style, making the same points as the original author.

That learned men are well known to disagree on this subject of punctuation is in itself a proof, that the knowledge of it, in theory and practice, is of some importance. I myself have learned by experience, that, if ideas that are difficult to understand are properly separated, they become clearer; and that, on the other hand, through defective punctuation, many passages are confused and distorted to such a degree, that sometimes they can with difficulty be understood, or even cannot be understood at all.
Aldus Manutius, *Interpungendi Ratio*, 1466.

The Moabite Stone, now in the Louvre, Paris, is the earliest known example of the use of punctuation.
© Photo R.M.N.

SPECIALIST LANGUAGE

Even though you may have a good working knowledge of the English Language – in other words, even though you speak it, read it and write it every day – it can still be a puzzle. Certain types of specialist language, for example, can seem totally foreign unless you are 'in the know'. Try the following examples:

What are the tribunal's functions under the Act? A tribunal has only three options under section 73: to grant an absolute discharge, to grant a conditional discharge or to refuse a discharge. The tribunal is exercising a judicial, as opposed to an administrative, function.

A judicial function does not of itself preclude the possibility of an adjournment to see whether or not conditions which are not then satisfied will be satisfied at some future date if that is within the scope of the powers given by the Act.

In his Lordship's judgment the Act did not give the tribunal any such powers. The tribunal had no such general supervisory function over the progress of a restricted patient. That was the function of the Home Secretary. The tribunal has certain specific judicial functions, namely to "direct the discharge of a patient . . . if they are satisfied . . . that he is not then suffering from mental illness."
Shiranikha Herbert, *The Guardian*, 29 October 1988

Black's second is an offbeat form of the unusual Nimzowitsch Defence, his third is already a mistake and possibly already the losing move. It is difficult to see how an experienced GM can employ such an opening against a strong opponent other than by a decision to 'take this little girl out of the books'.
4 . . . PxP   5 PxP N-K4
6 Q-K2 Q-K2   7 P-Q6!
An excellent pawn sacrifice which gains development time and lames both black bishops. A forced sequence now leads to an endgame where the grandmaster is already scrambling for survival.
1 P-K4 N-QB3   2 N-QB3 N-B3?!
3 P-Q4 P-K3?   4 P-Q5!
Leonard Barden, *The Guardian*, 29 October 1988

You will find more examples on the cassette and on Repromaster 24. *Is it easy to work out what each item refers to? On the repromaster you could underline in red the words or phrases which are new to you. Are there words that you recognise which appear to be used in a way that differs from the one you are used to?*

The more interested you become in a subject, the more involved you become with the language of the subject. As a beginner, though, you might have problems understanding the language used. Can you remember the first time you used a computer, or started a new hobby? Did you feel unsure of yourself, or even put off by the unfamiliar language?

● Using the simplest language, write a set of instructions for an activity that can be tested out in class: for example, fastening a tie, sharpening a pencil, changing the time on a digital watch. Read the examples below before you start.

The following sets of instructions were written by eleven-year-olds. Do they work out? What are the problems? What is missing?

How To Cut a Piece Of Paper With Scissors

Take a pair of scissors.
Hold them in your right hand.
Then put your right forefinger and thumb into the finger holes.
Then take a piece of paper in your left hand.
Then open the scissors by moving apart your finger and thumb.
Then place the edge of the paper into the 'V' shape made by the scissors.
Then close the scissors by bringing your finger and thumb together.
James

How To Draw a Straight Line

Take a piece of paper and place on a flat surface.
Then take a ruler and place it on top of the paper (flat side down).
Then take a pencil and hold it in between your forefinger and your thumb with the end touching the paper as well as touching the edge of the ruler.
Then bring the pencil towards you with it still touching the paper and the edge of the ruler.
Michelle

Below is a very famous send-up of the instructions for how to play a game. You might like to try to create a similar set of rules yourself.

The Rules of Cricket

You have two sides, one out in the field and one in.
Each man that's in the side that's in goes out and when he's out he comes in, and the next man goes in until he's out.
When they are all out the side that's out comes in, and the side that's been in goes out and tries to get those coming in out.
Sometimes you get men still in and not out.
When both sides have been in and out including the not outs that's the end of the game.
The M.C.C.

● Being as clear as you can with the language you use – and offering a glossary of definitions for those specialist words you can't avoid – prepare a 'Beginner's Guide to . . .' (You choose.) Perhaps it's a hobby or activity that you're very involved in. It could even be a beginner's guide to your school or to adolescence. Important elements might include a title page/contents page, a set of rules or instructions, diagrams/pictures/plans, an introduction, an account of your experiences, 'what the experts say' (you might interview your friends for this section), and so on. You could use the cut-ups provided on *Repromaster 25* to improve the presentation, if you like.

Have you, just for interest, looked at the instructions for any electrical goods that are presented in a number of languages? Try it now.

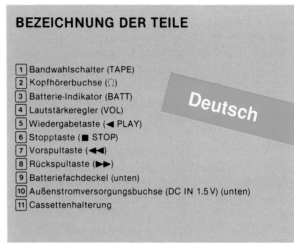

BEZEICHNUNG DER TEILE

1 Bandwahlschalter (TAPE)
2 Kopfhörerbuchse (Ω)
3 Batterie-Indikator (BATT)
4 Lautstärkeregler (VOL)
5 Wiedergabetaste (◄ PLAY)
6 Stopptaste (■ STOP)
7 Vorspultaste (◄◄)
8 Rückspultaste (►►)
9 Batteriefachdeckel (unten)
10 Außenstromversorgungsbuchse (DC IN 1.5 V) (unten)
11 Cassettenhalterung

Deutsch

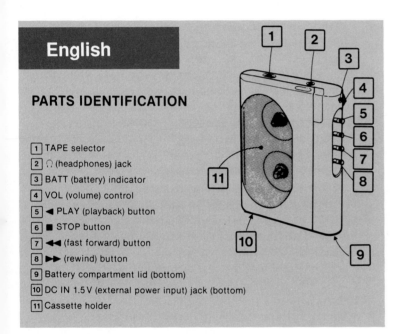

English

PARTS IDENTIFICATION

1 TAPE selector
2 Ω (headphones) jack
3 BATT (battery) indicator
4 VOL (volume) control
5 ◄ PLAY (playback) button
6 ■ STOP button
7 ◄◄ (fast forward) button
8 ►► (rewind) button
9 Battery compartment lid (bottom)
10 DC IN 1.5 V (external power input) jack (bottom)
11 Cassette holder

IDENTIFICACIÓN DE LAS PARTES

1 Selector de la cinta (TAPE)
2 Toma de auriculares (Ω)
3 Indicador del estado de la pila (BATT)
4 Control de volumen (VOL)
5 Botón de reproducción (◄ PLAY)
6 Botón de paro (■ STOP)
7 Botón de avance rápido (◄◄)
8 Botón de rebobinado (►►)
9 Tapa del compartimiento de la pila (parte inferior)
10 Toma de entrada de alimentación exterior (DC IN 1.5 V) (parte inferior)
11 Portacasete

Español

BENAMING VAN DE ONDERDELEN

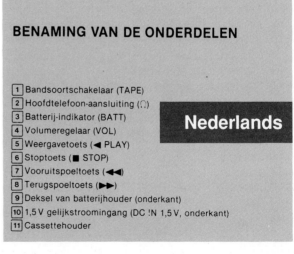

1 Bandsoortschakelaar (TAPE)
2 Hoofdtelefoon-aansluiting (Ω)
3 Batterij-indikator (BATT)
4 Volumeregelaar (VOL)
5 Weergavetoets (◄ PLAY)
6 Stoptoets (■ STOP)
7 Vooruitspoeltoets (◄◄)
8 Terugspoeltoets (►►)
9 Deksel van batterijhouder (onderkant)
10 1,5 V gelijkstroomingang (DC IN 1,5 V, onderkant)
11 Cassettehouder

Nederlands

IDENTIFICATIONS DES PARTIES

1 Sélecteur de bande (TAPE)
2 Prise de casque d'écoute (Ω)
3 Témoin de pile (BATT)
4 Réglage de volume (VOL)
5 Touche de lecture (◄ PLAY)
6 Touche d'arrêt (■ STOP)
7 Touche d'avance rapide (◄◄)
8 Touche de rebobinage (►►)
9 Couvercle de logement piles (sur le socle)
10 Prise d'entrée d'alimentation secteur (DC IN 1.5 V) (sur le socle)
11 Support cassette

Français

● What surprises you, when you compare? Which language(s) would appear to come closest to English?

CUT IT SHORT

Abbreviations have long been a feature of the English language. It is almost impossible to use a dictionary correctly without understanding them, and most good dictionaries have something in the region of twenty pages of common abbreviations as an appendix. In recent times they have begun to appear more and more. The most common everyday examples are to be found in newspaper advertisements.

The following is an example of abbreviation commonly used by estate agents to describe houses. Can you understand it?

BEDFORD GARDENS, W8
Imposing period fam. hse. beautifully interior designed with sth. facing gdn. Lnge. Din. Rm. Study. Kit./Brkfst. Rm. Mstr. Bed. Suite with Dress. Area/Bed. 6. 5 further Beds. 4 further Baths. 2 Clkrms. Util. Rm. Poss. parking. F/hold. £875,000. Sole Agents.

ONSLOW SQUARE, SW7
An elegant maisonette on gmd. and lwr. grnd. flrs. with enormous character. Draw. Rm. Ftd. Kit. Dble Bed. Mod. Bath. Storage Rm. Comm. gdns. C.H. Leasehold. £165,000.

● What are the advantages and disadvantages of communicating in this way? Draw up two lists – 'for' and 'against' abbreviations.

● Try advertising yourself and some of your friends in a similar way, reducing the descriptive and factual words to a minimum. Afterwards, discuss them with your group or class to decide how successful you were, and find out the common difficulties.

In George Orwell's science fiction novel **Nineteen Eighty-four**, *communication is in the process of being reduced to a minimum – for instance, in the society that Orwell describes, very few people write letters. Instead, printed postcards, with a few selected phrases to be crossed out or ticked off, are used. Interestingly enough, in recent years, fun postcards or greetings cards such as the one below, have appeared!*

● You might like to try and create a similar all-purpose card to send to someone, telling them how you did in your exams and what you intend to do when you leave school, for example.

Reducing the language to a minimum was a very serious business in Orwell's **Nineteen Eighty-four**. *It was to be done by command of the all-powerful leader of 'Oceania', 'Big Brother'. Here the main character, Winston, is enquiring about the development of a new dictionary of 'Newspeak', the name given to the new version of the language.*

"How is the Dictionary getting on?" said Winston, raising his voice to overcome the noise.

"Slowly," said Syme. "I'm on the adjectives. It's fascinating."

He had brightened up immediately at the mention of Newspeak. He pushed his pannikin aside, took up his hunk of bread in one delicate hand and his cheese in the other, and leaned across the table so as to be able to speak without shouting.

"The Eleventh Edition is the definitive edition," he said. "We're getting the language into its final shape – the shape it's going to have when nobody speaks anything else. When we've finished with it, people like you will have to learn it all over again. You think, I dare say, that our chief job is inventing new words. But not a bit of it! We're destroying words – scores of them, hundreds of them, every day. We're cutting the language down to the bone. The Eleventh Edition won't contain a single word that will become obsolete before the year 2050."

He bit hungrily into his bread and swallowed a couple of mouthfuls, then continued speaking, with a sort of pedant's passion. His thin dark face had become animated, his eyes had lost their mocking expression and grown almost dreamy.

"It's a beautiful thing, the destruction of words. Of course the great wastage is in the verbs and adjectives, but there are hundreds of nouns that can be got rid of as well. It isn't only the synonyms; there are also the antonyms. After all, what justification is there for a word which is simply the opposite of some other word? A word contains its opposite in itself. Take 'good' for instance. If you have a word like 'good', what need is there for a word like 'bad'? 'Ungood' will do just as well – better, because it's an exact opposite, which the other is not. Or again, if you want a stronger version of 'good', what sense is there in having a whole string of vague useless words like 'excellent' and 'splendid' and all the rest of them? 'Plusgood' covers the meaning; or 'doubleplusgood' if you want something stronger still. Of course we use those forms already, but in the final version of Newspeak there'll be nothing else. In the end the whole notion of goodness and badness will be covered by only six words – in reality, only one word. Don't you see the beauty of that, Winston?"

George Orwell, *Nineteen Eighty-four*

● Can you imagine why the language was being reduced in this way?

A general rule applied in 'Newspeak' is that any word in the language can be used either as a verb, noun, adjective or adverb – 'think' for example can be used for both 'think' and 'thought'. Adjectives are formed by adding '-ful' to the noun/verb, and adverbs are formed by adding '-wise'. (Speedful means rapid, speedwise means quickly.) As explained above, negatives are formed by adding 'un-'; more strength can by given by adding 'plus-', and even more strength by adding 'doubleplus-'. More examples would be: uncold = warm, pluscold = very cold, doublepluscold = absolutely freezing!

Options

● You might use Orwell's model for a language of the future as the basis of a piece of futuristic prose in which the characters use this form of communication.

● With a partner, take any two-page spread in a dictionary and reduce it. First discount any words *you* do not use. Then discount any words which you feel are not useful. Then form Orwellian adjectives, adverbs, negatives, opposites or superlatives for any remaining words.

The following is an example of a command in Newspeak for Winston to make alterations to a news article.

times 3.12.83 reporting bb dayorder doubleplusungood refs unpersons rewrite fullwise upsub antefiling

In Oldspeak (or standard English) this might be rendered:

The reporting of Big Brother's Order for the Day in *The Times* of December 3rd 1983 is extremely unsatisfactory and makes references to non-existent persons. Rewrite it in full and submit your draft to higher authority before filing.

● Take a newspaper and change as many of the headlines as you can into Newspeak. You might even tackle short news stories or even produce your own Newspeak newspaper.

Two ancient forms of poetry from Japan, Senryu and Haiku, are very short and have very strict rules. The first line must have five syllables, the second seven syllables and the third five syllables. Senryu usually deals with common or humorous incidents. Traditional Haiku, as can be seen from the example below, always contains some reference to nature and is concerned with a particular moment in time.

Constancy

Though it be broken –
broken again – still it's there:
– moon on the water.
Choshu

The form can of course be used to deal with any subject effectively, as can be seen from the examples written by young people below:

Silence

Billy, it's quiet
Whispers John through the night sky.
Then the siren goes.

Why? is the question,
As he buries his partner,
Crying in his hands.

Robert Pickering

Fish Out of Water

Fish out of water
Some people would not reach out
But I tried, I tried.

Laura Doyle

A very recent idea, the Mini-saga, was devised for a national competition a few years ago. Entries had to be exactly fifty words long (not including the title) and they had to tell a story that showed the passage of time. Below are two examples:

The Reason of Man and the Instinct of the Beast

A woodsman lived in a cottage with his baby. By day he hewed timber, his trusted Alsatian guarding the infant. One evening he found turmoil, the cot overturned, the dog with bloodied muzzle. He shot it. A muffled whimper followed from the unharmed child. Nearby lay a dead Siberian wolf.
Jonathan Stoker

Converted

The lion gazed dreamily at its cut paw. What a nice man, that missionary, who, on hearing the moans, had fearlessly come over and pulled out the thorn. The lion smiled lazily as it licked the missionary's boots – a little tough, perhaps, but the rest had certainly been very tender.
Jack Union

● Now produce your own Haiku, Senryu or Mini-saga. You could combine them into a class anthology.

THE FUTURE OF LANGUAGE

Language continues to change and develop constantly for a wide variety of reasons. Languages still borrow from each other: for example, you might expect to hear man-shon (mansion), and aisu-kurimu (ice cream) in Japan; and seksapil (sex appeal) and non-khau (know-how) in Russia. The humorist and writer, Miles Kington, has taken this idea to amusing lengths in a series of books entitled **Let's Parler Franglais.** *What is interesting is that his comic invention is coming nearer and nearer to the truth!*

Lesson Trente-Huit: Le Shoplifting

DÉTECTIVE: Ah ha! Gotchère!

MADAME: Squark!

DÉTECTIVE: Vous êtes nabbée. Je vous ai attrapée avec les mains rouges. C'est un cop blond, n'est-ce pas?

MADAME: Ah, monsieur, ayez pitié, et donnex-moi un break. Je suis une petite old lady, j'habite dans une chambre condamnée et je n'ai qu'un seul ami: mon chat Biggs. C'est pour lui, ce tin de tuna chunks.

DÉTECTIVE: C'est extravagant, le tuna. Pourquoi pas les pilchards?

MADAME: Les pilchards sont sur le top shelf. Je suis une très petite old lady.

DÉTECTIVE: Bon point.

MADAME: Et aussi, si vous êtes un shoplifteur, le tuna est le même prix que les pilchards.

DÉTECTIVE: C'est vrai. En ce cas, pourquoi pas le caviar?

MADAME: Biggs déteste le caviar.

DÉTECTIVE: Hmm . . . Nous semblons avoir perdu le drift. Recommencons . . . Ah ha! Gotchère! Vous êtes nabbée! Venez avec moi chez le Deputy Manager!

MADAME: Un moment. Avez-vous identification? Un proof que vous êtes détective de store?

DÉTECTIVE: Volontiers. Voilà ma carte: 'J. Wisbech est appointé détective de store par Waffle et Peabody, le plus grand store départmental de Londres de sud, late night jeudi, est. 1879.'

MADAME: Bon. Et voilà ma carte. 'Ruth Gingold est une membre certifiée des Shoplifteurs Internationals, Paris, Melbourne et Nouveau York, le guild global pour l'improvement des standards de shoplifting.'

DÉTECTIVE: C'est un leg-pull ou quoi?

MADAME: Non, c'est mort sérieux. Nous faisons un filme documentaire sur le shoplifting et espécialement sur les petites old ladies qui habitent dans une seule chambre avec leur chat, Biggs. C'est pour le BBC-Deux, avec backing de Temps-Vie, Interpol, et Oceanfresh Tuna Chunks.

DÉTECTIVE: Vous m'invitez à croire que nous sommes dans un *filme*?

MADAME: Mais oui. Regardez, les caméras.

DÉTECTIVE: Mon dieu, c'est vrai!

MADAME: Merci pour votre co-opération, M. Wisbech. Incidentellement, vous êtes plus grand que moi. Si vous pouvez me passer un tin de pilchards . . .

DÉTECTIVE: Voilà.

MADAME: Merci. Maintenant, je dois être sur ma route. Au revoir.

DÉTECTIVE: Au revoir . . . Une charmante vieille dame. Un moment! Ces caméras sont les caméras a circuit-fermé de Waffle et Peabody! Ah, on m'a pris pour un ride! Stop, voleur! Stop, voleur . . . !

Miles Kington, *Parlez-Vous Franglais?*

His main technique is to use English colloquialisms (everyday, informal phrases such as 'you're pulling my leg' or 'it's a fair cop') and translate them literally into French with the odd English word for good measure.

● Can you work out all the colloquialisms in the piece above? Try 'tampering' with some English colloquialisms yourself, and translating them into French. You could even try a piece of 'Franglais' roleplay if you're really clever . . . a group of English tourists on a day trip to France?

More serious attempts have been made to cross international boundaries by means of international languages. These include Volapuk, Glossa, Ido and up to six hundred more. Of these, Esperanto is undoubtedly the most successful. The language was first published in 1887 and it is currently used by more than ten million people. Esperantists have their own associations, books and magazines. It is claimed that Esperanto is five times easier to learn than any other language. It looks like this:

'Esperanto estas tre facile lernebla lingvo sed povas tute plenumi la funkciojn de iu ajn etnika lingvo'. ('Esperanto is a very easily learnable language but [it] can completely fulfil the functions of any ethnic language.')

● Discuss the advantages and disadvantages of such a development in language.

The spread of the English language has been dramatic. In some parts of the world, however, English is becoming so well blended with various other languages that new, almost unrecognisable languages are being formed. This is occurring most noticeably in parts of Africa and India, and in Singapore ('Singlish'). Perhaps the most dramatic development is that of 'Nation Language' in the Caribbean. Many Caribbean writers (most notably the 'dub poets') are in the forefront in promoting Nation Language. The following extract explains how and why:

They are turning their backs on Standard English out of choice. They have chosen to write in the language of their own culture, and to disseminate it throughout the English-speaking world in performance, records, tapes and books. They are extremely alert to the idea that the language of their poetry might become the future standard language of the Caribbean and give their society a distinct

Caribbean identity that is not overshadowed by English or American English. Edward Brathwaite likes to make the point, in talking about English in the Caribbean, that the Third World as a whole is "accutely concerned with language". As he says, "We regard words, word play, word power, as an essential part of our personality." The question of the meaning and significance of those words, and the kind of words they should be, is fundamental to all the New Englishes.

The debate has changed as the political language has changed. In the 1950s before the Caribbean had achieved independence from Britain the emphasis on Standard English was oppressive. Brathwaite recalls the experience of the law courts. "The judge would expect the defendant to speak as best he could in the Queen's English. This would come out as broken English and the man would be hesitant and embarrassed. Now, with the acceptance of the nation language, the defendant comes in dressed as he is, and speaks to the judge as himself, and is much more eloquent, and much more successful in his dealings with the court."

Brathwaite believes that Bob Marley achieved a great deal for 'nation language'. In his lifetime Marley was without doubt the most famous West Indian in the world, invited as guest of honour to Independence Day celebrations and peace rallies. His music swept Britain and the United States, influencing a generation of songwriters. His lyrics gave poignant expression to the Caribbean predicament: an imposed identity that is neither African nor European nor American. His worldwide success gave Jamaican creole international credibility. "I notice now," Brathwaite says, "that announcers on the radio are quite happy to move into nation language." In school, the trend towards a Caribbean English is emphasised by the emergence of examinations devised and adjudicated not in London (as previously), but in the Caribbean.

In the university, the movement towards nation language or Jamaican creole has taken a radical direction. One of the leading spokesmen for the recognition of Jamaican creole is Dr Hubert Devonish, a Guyanese. For him, "the major struggle right now is to fight for the government to recognise that Jamaican creole is as worthy of attention and respect as English." He sees Jamaican creole as "a very old language that the slaves brought from Africa to the Caribbean." He points out that historically it has *always* been on a path of development that is quite different from English. Devonish argues that though the

African slaves picked up the vocabulary of English, they retained the grammatical structure of their African languages. No one, he says, can overlook the fact that the structure of all the Caribbean creoles – English, Dutch, French and Spanish – is very similar. "My argument," he says, "is that from a historical and linguistic point of view you're dealing with a separate language."

Devonish argues that English is the language of an elite, cut off from the mass of the Caribbean population. If the people of Jamaica are to participate fully in their society the government should recognise Jamaican creole as an official – and separate – language. "There is," says Devonish, "no reason why any elite group within Jamaican society should determine that only one language, that of the dominant European power, should be the official language."

Robert McCrum, William Cran & Robert MacNeil,
The Story of English

Options

● Make a list of the strongest statements made in the passage about Nation Language and Jamaican creole. Discuss with your group why the recognition of Nation Language is important for the people of the Caribbean. Report your ideas back to the class.

● The Chief Editor of the *Oxford English Dictionary*, Dr Robert Burchfield, suggested in the late seventies that over the next few centuries English will have disintegrated into many different languages. Will we see the kind of blurring of the edges humorously suggested by Miles Kington or the development of numerous 'Nation Languages' owing at least part of their roots to English? Or will we see the development of a world language such as Esperanto? What do you think?

DOE MEIN ICE DESLEEVE ME?

All the unusual words in the following piece of writing are no longer in use. It is unlikely, then, that you will understand what it means! However, the fact that you understand the way in which words are used means that you may be able to answer the questions below.

The blonke was maily, like all the others. Unlike the other blonkes, however, it had spiss crinet completely covering its fairney cloots and concealing, just below one of them, a small wam.

This particular blonke was quite drumly – lennow, in fact, and almost samded. When yerden, it did not quetch like the other blonkes, or even blore. The others blored very readily.

It was probably his bellytimber that had made the one blonke so drumly. The bellytimber was quite kexy, had a strong shawk, and was apparently venenated. There was only one thing to do with the venenated bellytimber: givel it in the flosh. This would be much better than to sparple it in the wong, since the blonkes that were not drumly could icchen in the wong, but not in the flosh.

Questions

1. Where was the small wam?
2. Why weren't the other blonkes drumly?
3. If bellytimber is venenated, is it wise to givel it in the flosh?

Below are the meanings of the words used so that you can 'crack the code' and translate the whole passage.

Bellytimber Food, provisions
Blonke A large, powerful horse
Blore To cry out or bleat and bray like an animal
Crinet A hair
Drumly Cloudy, sluggish
Fairney Cloots Small horny substances above the hoofs of horses, sheep and goats.
Flosh A swamp or stagnant pool overgrown with weeds
Givel To heap up
Icchen To move, stir
Kexy Dry, juiceless
Lennow Floppy, limp
Maily Speckled
Quetch To moan and twitch in pain, shake
Samded Half-dead
Shawk Smell
Sparple To scatter, spread about
Spiss Thick, dense
Venenate To poison
Wam A scar, cicatrix
Wong Meadowlands, commons
Yerd To beat with a rod.

● Referring to the list of 'lost words' on *Repromaster 26* produce your own paragraph similar to the one above, using the words in the correct context. Then prepare a list of questions for another person/group to answer, about the content of the passage.

John Lennon enjoyed playing with language, and created short stories and poems like the one below. In this case, the words are perhaps easier to understand as there is usually some similarity between them and 'real' words.

Silly Norman

"I really don't know woot tow mak of these," said Norman, as he sorted through him Chrimbas posed. "It seem woot I git mower litters und parskels than woot I know peoples, it suplizes moi moor et moor each yar, as moor on these pareskle keep cooming. I really doon't knaw whew all they body are – seddling ik all this." He clab quitely too the fire, sheving a few mough ruddish awn. "It's came tow a pretty parse when I don't evil knew where they cam frog." Norman coop an stetty keel and prumptly wed intow thee kitcheon tow put up thee kettle orn. "I might as welsh mak me a copper tea, I night as welp hev a chcolush birskit as well, wile I do noddy." So saying so he marshed offer to that teapod and tap it to that sing: bud to he grey suffise – what! – bat noo warty. "Goob heralds! what's all of thiz goinge awn? Doe mein ice desleeve me? Am I knot loofing at me owen sing-unice, and there be know warty?" He was quait raight, lo! the warty didn noo apear, trey as he maybe.

Off course we all know whey this warty do no coomb, becourgh the tangs they are awl freezup, awl on they, awl they freezop. Norman dig knort know that, for Norman him a silly man – yes – Norman is sorft. "OH deally meat! oh woe isme, wart canada, ther are nay werters toe mick a caper tay, ange me moover she arther cooming ferty too. I shall heave two gough nextador, perhats they might hall hefty." Sow Norman he gentry poots his had hand coat orn makeing sewer to wrave hisself op like he moomy tell him, broosh beyond the ears and out of that frant door he ghost. To him try amasemaid, he fainds nought a houfe nought a hough inside! Wart on earth is heffering? – why – there iznot a hug tobeseen, not anyway fer miles aboot. "Goody Griff, which artery in HEFFER harold be they norm! is these not thet enid of the worm? Surely to goosestep I am nit that larst man on earn?" he fell suddy to the ground weefy and whaley crizeling tuber Lawn abooue to savfre him or judge spare a friend or to. "I wilf give of awl my wordy posesions, awl me foren stabs, awl me classicow rechords, awl me fave rave pidgeons of Humpty Littlesod thee great nothing. All these oh wondrouse Sailor up above, I offer ye if only yer will save me!"

Normans mather, who you remembrane, was a combing tooty, was shorked when she cam acroose him lyinge awn the floor thus crying. "My dear NORMAN!" she screege, "Wart in Griff's nave are you doing, why are you carroling on this way?" She wogged slightly over to her own son, with a woddied loof in her eye. "Police don't garryon like this my son, tell Muddle werts the metre." Norman raved himself slowly and sabbly locked at her. "Carrot you see, mubber, Griff have end the worled. I only went to guess sam warty, and then it dibble wirk, so I went to go necktie to a nebough and I saw wit had happened – GRIFF had ended the worl. I saw nothing – every where there where no neybers. Oh Mather wet is happening?" Normans mither take won loog at he with a disabeleafed spression on her head. "My Golf! Norman wit are yuo torking about turn? Donald you member thet there have been nobodys livfing here ever? Rememble whensday first move in how you say – 'Thank Heavy there are no peoplre about this place, I want to be aloef?' have you fergit all thistle?"

Norman lucked op at he mam (stikl cryling) with teeth in his eye, saying – "Muther, thou art the one, the power ov atterny, for heavan sakes amen. Thank you dear mether, I had truly forgot. I am a silly Norman!" They booth link arbs and walk brightly to the house.

"Fancy me ferbetting that no-bottle lives roynd here mother! Fantasie forgetting thet!" They each laff together as they head four the kitchenn – and lo! – that warty runs again, the sunbeefs had done it, and they booth have tea, booth on them. Which jub shaw yer –

'However blackpool tower maybe,
In time they'll bassaway.
Have faith and trumpand B B C –
Griffs' light make bright your day.'
AMEN (and mickaela dentist.)

John Lennon

Options

● Have fun with language: with a partner create a few new words of your own and then present to the class a performance of a weather forecast or a party political broadcast, a news bulletin or a cookery demonstration. Create, in other words, a new specialist vocabulary for the subject you will be presenting.

● Very young children particularly seem to like 'nonsense' verse. *Jabberwocky* by Lewis Carroll is a very famous example. Can you explain the appeal? You might like to ask younger brothers or sisters or children from your local infant school what they think.

● Several years ago a children's programme called *The Flowerpot Men* was criticised for the 'nonsense way' the puppet characters talked. Do you think there could be possible harm in exposing children to nonsense language? After group discussion you could roleplay the situation in which the producer of a programme like *The Flowerpot Men* is answering the criticisms of a parent.

● Produce a questionnaire for parents at a local playgroup or mother-and-toddler group, or the parents of infant school children, on various aspects of children's television. What is their opinion of 'nonsense talk', for example? Write up your findings in a report.

VARIATIONS

Gust Becos I Cud Not Spel

Gust becos I cud not spel
It did not mean I was daft
When the boys in school red my riting
Some of them laffed

But now I am the dictater
They have to rite like me
Utherwise they cannot pas
Ther GCSE

Some of the girls wer ok
But those who laffed a lot
Have al bean rownded up
And hav recintly bean shot

The teecher who corrected my spelling
As not been shot at al
But four the last fifteen howers
As bean standing up against a wal

He has to stand ther until he can spel
Figgymisgrugifooniyn the rite way
I think he will stand ther forever
I just inventid it today
Alan Ahlberg

Typewriting Class

Dear Miss Hinson
I am spitting
In front of my top ratter
With the rest of my commercesnail sturdy students
Triping you this later.
The truce is Miss Hinson
I am not happy wiht my cross.
Every day on Woundsday
I sit in my dusk
with my type rutter
Trooping without lurking at the lattice
All sorts of weird messengers.
To give one exam pill,
'The quick down socks ...
The quick brine pox ...
The sick frown box ...
The sick down jocks
Humps over the hazy bog'
When everyone knows
That a sick down jock
Would not be seen dead
Near a hazy bog.
Another one we tripe is;
'Now is the tame
For all guide men
To cram to the head
Of the pratty.'
To may why of sinking
I that is all you get to tripe
In true whelks of sturdy
Then I am thinking of changing
To crookery classes.
I would sooner end up a crook
Than a shirt hand trappist
Any die of the wink.
I have taken the tremble, Miss Hinson
To trip you this later
So that you will be able
To understand my indignation.
I must clothe now
As the Bill is groaning.

Gareth Owen

A Good English Recipe

Take a blank page
Cover it with writing
Dot it with full stops,
Sprinkle with commas
Add a few apostrophes,
A splash of speech marks
Mix in the metaphors,
Season with similes
Pour in a little personification
Arrange the adjectives,
And knead in the nouns.
Cream in the question marks.
Enter in the verbs
Dice it and spice it with added adverbs
Throw in pickled pronouns
Stir in sentences
Mix it with skill
Divide into paragraphs
Test for spellings
And bake it with care.
Present neatly finished
Cap it with capitals
Decorate with a date and a title to match,
Serve to whoever wants to read it.
Linda Dowse

Writing

and then i saw it
saw it all all the mess
and blood and evrythink
and mam agenst the kichin dor
the flor all stiky
and the wall all wet
and red an dad besid the kichen draw
i saw it saw it all
an wrot it down an ever word of it is tru

You must take care to write in sentences.
Check your spellings and your paragraphs.
Is this finished? It is rather short.
Perhaps next time you will have more to say.
Jan Dean

Private? No!

Punctuation can make a difference.
            Private
        No swimming
          Allowed

does not mean the same as
            Private?
        No. Swimming
          Allowed.
Willard R. Espy

Jabberwocky

'Twas brillig, and the slithy toves
    Did gyre and gimble in the wabe;
All mimsy were the borogoves
    And the mome raths outgrabe.

'Beware the Jabberwock, my son!
    The jaws that bite, the claws that catch!
Beware the Jubjub bird, and shun
    The frumious Bandersnatch!'

He took his vorpal sword in hand:
    Long time the manxome foe he sought –
So rested he by the Tumtum tree,
    And stood awhile in thought.

And as in uffish thought he stood,
    The Jabberwock, with eyes of flame,
Came whiffling through the tulgey wood,
    And burbled as it came!

One, two! One, two! And through and through
    The vorpal blade went snicker-snack!
He left it dead, and with its head
    He went galumphing back.

'And hast thou slain the Jabberwock?
    Come to my arms, my beamish boy!
O frabjous day! Callooh! Callay!'
    He chortled in his joy.

'Twas brillig, and the slithy toves
    Did gyre and gimble in the wabe;
All mimsy were the borogoves,
    And the mome raths outgrabe.
Lewis Carroll

TAKING THE REGISTER

WRITING FOR CHILDREN

Countless numbers of authors have written with one audience in mind – children. Perhaps the names of Beatrix Potter, A. A. Milne and the Reverend W. E. Awdry are not quite as well known as their creations Peter Rabbit, Winnie the Pooh and Thomas the Tank Engine, but these are amongst the most popular writers of children's stories. To capture the imagination of young children is quite an art, and to write well for an audience many years younger than yourself requires great skill.

Very careful consideration of the types of books that used to interest, excite or amuse you may help you to understand all the elements that go to make a good children's story.

Options

● What stories were told to you as a child? Did you have favourites? Did any leave a particularly strong or lasting impression? Make a list. What made them appeal to you? Was it the settings? The characters? The adventures? The humour? The excitement? Make a chart like this to record your ideas.

TITLE	What I liked about the book: Characters	Settings	Humour	Excitement	Pictu

● Now discuss your thoughts with a partner. Make a note of the ideas/memories you have shared.

● Then look through any children's books you can find ... in the classroom, in your local library or at home.

● Select six or more and think about why they appeal to you. Is it the language (simple, unusual, poetic, etc.)? Is it the storyline (easy to follow, exciting, amusing, etc.)? Is it the emotions (humour, sadness, fear, bravery)? Is it the characters (amazing, naughty, like you, the opposite of you, fantastic or impossible)? Is it the message or the moral? (Does the story explore difficult situations or overturn old ideas?) Is it the endings (happy, unexpected)? Is it the illustrations? (Do they add to the story?) And so on. Add your own ideas. List your responses as shown below.

TITLE	Language	Storyline	Characters	Emoti

● Discuss your responses with at least two other people, who should have covered different books/stories from yours. One question you might discuss is how children's tastes in stories change as they get older. Are there particular styles of writing, subjects or types of characters that have particular appeal for certain age groups?

● Now write up your findings from what you've done so far under the title 'Children's books: some memories and opinions'.

● Now rough out a story of your own, having decided what age group you're going for. Use big sheets of paper and prepare a mock-up when your story is complete.

● Try out several ideas before you make your final decision. Read them to your small group. Keep a record – a 'writer's diary' where you jot down your thoughts and feelings about creating the story. Is it harder than you thought? What are the major problems? Describe the re-drafting process.

● Once you have come up with your final story, test it out once more on your group. If you have younger brothers or sisters, they could be a suitable audience. Then write it all up, taking care to illustrate your story attractively (you could get a younger child to produce illustrations). Before you send it off to your local infant or junior school, prepare a simple questionnaire (or use the response sheet on *Repromaster 28*) which will allow the child, possibly with an adult helping, to respond to your story.

● Well, what did they think? Do you believe their criticism and/or praise to be justified?

● Write a short piece about what you have learned from the whole experience.

SOMETHING TO WRITE HOME ABOUT ...

When schools produce pieces of writing for adults (your parents, to be precise) and the purpose of whatever is being written is to communicate information, the style of writing is often very formal, as in the examples on this page. What do you think of these examples? Are they too formal and business-like, or are they appropriate? Which are the least and most formal? How do they compare with examples from your own school? What are the hidden messages behind the words – what is the school trying to communicate about itself?

Dear Parent,
Your son/daughter *Amjad*
will be required to stay behind until 4.30 pm on *Wednesday*
7th October for *Being badly behaved in lesson*
I would be grateful for your cooperation in this matter which
we consider to be very important.
If your child is unable to stay behind on this occasion,
please contact school to make other arrangements.
Yours sincerely
M. Hanison
Headmaster
Deputy Headmaster

Detention given by *Mr. Bailey*

*Delete where applicable

* I give/do not give permission for my son/daughter *Amjad*
to stay for detention on
7th October
signed *M Khaleen* Parent/(Guardian)
Date *6th October*

Dear *Mr. Atkinson*
I am writing to let you know that *Diana*
left school without permission on *Friday 7th April*
Since this behaviour amounts to truancy I have
placed *her* on attendance report for this
week. I trust that this will be a lesson to
as he/she was "caught out" immediately and knows
that I am writing to you. I shall not be taking
any further action on this occasion. However, if
you would like to contact me regarding this, or
any other matter, I would be happy to discuss it
with you.

Yours sincerely
Khalid Mirza

Options

● Write your own versions of similar letters in what, in your opinion, is an effective and appropriate style.

● Would this be an appropriate response to a letter from school?

Dear *Mr. Devlin*
Your son/daughter *Lesley* was absent from
school from *April 28th* *April 30th* and,
according to our records, we have received no
note or telephone call from you explaining this.
Would you please fill in the slip below stating
the reason for this absence and return this
letter to the headmaster for the attention
of *Mr Curran*

Yours faithfully *R Smith*

I have spoken with my daughter about this
matter; at first she denied it, but then admitted
that she had absented herself. She has been
told she cannot go out for a month and instructed
to apologise to the teacher concerned.

Signed: *D Devlin* (Parent/Guardian)

Date: *May 2nd*

Dear _____
My son/daughter was absent from school
on _____ due to _____
We have/have not consulted the doctor on this
occasion.
I would be grateful if you would extend our
apologies to _____
for any inconvenience caused and express our
gratitude to _____
for his/her/their concern
Yours sincerely/faithfully
_____

● Write a series of official/formal letters from school with similar official/formal replies from home, producing a humorous exchange of correspondence.

● Write a story about a young person, told entirely through a series of official school letters.

- Examine the language used on your latest school report and consider the question, 'Are the comments totally honest and factual?' (You could ask your group or even discuss it with your teacher.)

- Imagine that you are not an ideal pupil; fill in a report for yourself using the repromaster blank (*Repromaster 29*), disguising the truth.

- For what purposes are you given letters to take home concerning other aspects of school life? In what ways do the styles differ? What are the reasons for the difference? Should they be different? Examine examples of such letters. What clues do they contain about the different types of messages the writer is trying to communicate?

What do you feel about the example below, written by a headteacher of a primary school to parents? What messages are being communicated? What kind of relationship is the writer trying to build with the reader? What clues are there?

Dear Parents,

Very soon your child, with others, will be starting school, and in order that they may settle quickly and happily in the new environment, I hope you will not mind if I make a few suggestions, with most of which I am sure you are already familiar.

Talk often to your child about this new adventure – never threaten with school. Make sure that you tell them how you will miss them while they are away. Tell them the kind of things you will be busy doing in their absence – cooking, making beds, etc. Assure them that you will be missing them and awaiting their return, and that every care will be taken of their toys and things in their absence. It is dismaying if smaller brothers or sisters are allowed to spoil their toys whilst they are away at school.

Don't be alarmed if, during the first few weeks, there is a sudden breakdown, and your child becomes clinging and doesn't want to be left. Just talk in a reassuring manner and make your departure quickly. Tell the child at what time you will return. I can assure you that if the distress was very real and lasting I should get in touch with you. If you have said that you will be waiting at the gate, make sure you are there – a little child can feel that mother will never again appear if this promise is broken.

I shall probably suggest, if it is feasible, that your child comes in the morning only, or for an even shorter time. Some children find a full school day too much at first, and if we work together we can gradually lengthen this period. Not all children need this form of introduction to school life. If children have been used to leaving mother, and have had lots of contact with other children, they will settle much more quickly. I shall write to you suggesting times for a preschool visit – please try to come and stay with your child. Here is a chance for you to share their new experiences.

If children can cope with all their garments (these should be clearly marked) it helps to make the settling in process much more simple. Most children can, of course, cope with their own toilet needs, and can ask in recognisable terms when they need to visit the toilet.

Often parents ask what they can do about children reading and writing before they come to school. Rarely is a child ready to do any formal learning before starting school, but talking with them and having books available is of immense value. I know you will have all read to your children and allowed them to use pencils and crayons. Counting games are fun, and a great help to us when they begin to learn.

Now for a little about our school. I know many of you will be told by your children that 'we played all day'. Let me assure you that this is not really so. At this early stage the things we want them to learn are presented in a play fashion. To a small child play is work, and we know that you will find yourself surprised what a great deal of knowledge your child is absorbing and learning in this way.

We try to give each child the minimum time of eighteen months with his first teacher. We have found constant change of teacher, who at this stage must be the mother's substitute, is very harmful to the child's progress.

I also want to emphasise that I am here at any time to answer your queries. It helps the school and the child to know of any changes at home which may have disturbed them. Never feel that any problem is too small for you to consult us about. It is only by working together and knowing each other well that we can make sure that every child is a happy, confident, secure little individual, growing up to be a valued member of the community.

Yours faithfully,
MARGARET J. WRIGHT
Head Mistress

A MANNER OF SPEAKING

● Listen to the tape of young people discussing the way they talk.

I do have different ways of speaking in different situations: sometimes I will shout and scream at my brother, then the phone will ring, for me, and automatically my harsh, common voice will change to a friendly subtle voice. I think people's voices influence you very much. Sometimes phrases go round and people will pick them up; soon the whole class will be using one person's catchphrase. I really hate my voice, I have a very broad accent and when taping it, it disgusts me. I think, "Is that my voice?" and get embarrassed. I hate people who swear all the time, it sounds vulgar and common. I talk differently to different people, this is perhaps something everyone does, but when I am angry I just lose control and everything I have been holding back comes tumbling out in a tangled mess.

The only time I am uncertain of myself is when I am talking either to a grown-up or to a boyfriend. I always seem to talk too much, and say something I shouldn't. When I have been told off by my dad (which is very often) he never lets me get a word in edgeways. He usually blows his top and screams at me, saying "Get to bed!" or "Grounded!" Then I'll just storm off in a rage. Over the years my voice has changed very little. I have a few annoying habits like saying, "Yes, yes," when someone's lecturing me. I am very lucky though, because I can talk to anyone. People say I have the 'gift of the gab'. Do I think it's true? Maybe.
Suzanne

I speak in many different ways. For example, when I answer the phone for my mum or dad and it's for them, I tend to put on a more relaxed, posh sort of voice. If I am talking to a person I have just been introduced to I would talk normally and pick my words carefully. When I was on holiday once, we got talking to a family from Birmingham. They commented on our accent, especially mine, being a young Yorkshire lad, and how nice it was.

I never seem to be uncertain when I'm speaking, except when I'm reading in class. Many people comment on my voice and some say it is quite high pitched, so sometimes I disguise that by putting on a deeper voice. But now my voice has changed to a deeper tone, and so I don't have to disguise it.

There are many times when I want to say something but it won't come out. Like when I'm in an argument or something similar, I try to say what I feel but I cannot put it into words.
Craig

I do not like my accent so I try to speak better when I am with people I hardly know and I also talk better when I am trying to impress people.
Samantha

I recently moved from one area of the town to another and was amazed at the different dialects within the districts. I found I could understand people quite easily but the occasional word would confuse me. The same words meant totally different things in the two areas. I was conscious of this fact until I began to pick up the local slang words. Now I do not even think about the way I talk when I am with friends.

Jane

My dad used to tell me to speak louder but I still speak quietly and when I speak to people I don't really look straight at them, except with my family and friends.

When I speak with my friends I talk the same as I talk with my parents, except I swear sometimes.

Sometimes I think my voice is 'out of tune' and it sounds funny. In an argument I never choose my words properly and after an argument I always think, ''Oh, I wish I'd said that.''

Zoë

When I am talking to my grandparents or someone I have just been introduced to, then I talk a bit slower or clearer so they can hear what I say properly. My mother talks Grenadian when she's shouting. She uses the odd phrase now and then but never when we are talking normally. My father just talks Jamaican when he's messing about. I only talk Jamaican when I am messing about with my friends. I don't like talking much when I go to my relatives down in London, because when I speak the people make fun of my accent. So I have to talk a lot plainer and louder for them to understand. When I'm talking to my friends they often say that I talk too fast and mumble a lot so they tell me to slow down and talk louder, which irritates me a lot.

Delroy

The language I speak most is English and many people find that hard to believe because my parents are originally from India. I find the only time I speak Punjabi is with the older generation like my grandparents, who don't understand English. I find it difficult sometimes to talk in Punjabi as it is only once in a while that I talk in this language. My grandparents feel that I should know more about my background and one day should visit India but I don't know why. I have no interest in visiting the Punjab. I have no reading or writing skills in the language and only just about scrape by speaking. I have never talked to my parents in Punjabi, or with friends or relatives of my age.

Vinnie

Options

How I talk

● In a small group pick out the points from these pieces of writing that you can identify in yourself. See if others agree.

● What other interesting aspects of the way you talk can you think of? Report back.

Family talk

● Generate a piece of research at home. Do your parents talk to you differently at home and in public? Do they talk in different ways when addressing each other, close friends, neighbours, strangers, other members of the family? If you have brothers or sisters, how does their style of talking vary from occasion to occasion? Are there any situations in which your family's combined style of talking changes completely? Are there any particular words or phrases you or your family use repeatedly?

● Either write up an account of the way you talk;
or write up your observations of 'family talk';
or combine your two pieces of study into a personal account, entitled 'A Manner of Speaking'.

● Produce a piece of drama-script based on a family incident, real or imaginary. Make it as true to life as you can.

INTENDED AUDIENCE

You are probably the best audience you are ever likely to get. You can talk to yourself in any way you wish, and say whatever you like without fear of offending anyone.

Get Your Audience Right

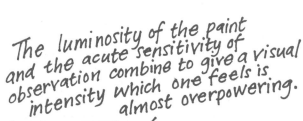

● Write a 'stream of consciousness' piece (a piece of writing which you do without pausing or thinking about what you are going to write next) addressed to yourself directly and with only you as the intended audience. The subject of your writing will be just what kind of person, in your opinion, you really are. Write about how you behave at home with your family, at school with your teachers and with your friends. Write about the kind of personality you have – whether you are witty, kind, generous, jealous, lively, dull, easily upset and so on. Examine what you have written. In what ways would the way you express your thoughts and feelings differ if you were talking with your best friend about the subject? With a parent? With your careers teacher? With a prospective employer? Write a few sentences for each. Clearly the subject remains the same, but your presentation will vary because of your intended audience.

The amount of information an audience already has about the subject (in the above example – you) will significantly affect the way any new information is delivered. Who is the intended audience for each of the following articles?

'Education for All: A New Approach.' The essence of this, the most important chapter of all is to articulate the need for educating *all* children to understand and appreciate the multi-cultural nature of society. To this end overt and institutional racism must be identified and countered in the strongest possible terms. The need for a multi-cultural perspective to permeate all aspects of school life is firmly stressed, the responsibility for which is placed in the hands of the entire education system, from the D.E.S., through H.M.I. to L.E.A.s, their advisory services, down to schools. Schools, with guidance from their L.E.A., must formulate, and implement, clear policies designed to combat racism and ensure 'Education for All'. The S.C.D.C. has also been directed towards a reappraisal of existing materials. Examination boards, like teachers, have been asked to ensure their syllabi/curricula accurately and positively reflect the multi-cultural nature of society.

The contention is that the innovator, deploying whichever strategy he may choose, is in need of guidelines to prevent him from being swallowed up whole. To begin with, the general approach demands that the would-be innovator possesses a more systems-orientated view of the entire organisation, rather than a view that he is dealing with individual clients. Does he possess a realistic appreciation of the true scale required for change within his organisation and an appreciation of the need to strike and maintain the right tempo? Is he generally taking into account the needs of *all* others involved in the system?

● Using the example on *Repromaster 30* – or any other short piece of 'specialist writing' you can find – mark those items which show that the intended audience has previous information on the subject – that is, those phrases and individual words which you feel are directly connected to the subject of the article and which may be unfamiliar to you.

The same basic information is often transmitted in a variety of ways depending upon the intended audience. In the case, for example, of journalists, a very clear picture of the reader – what the reader already knows, what they are likely to want to know and in what style they would like it delivered – is of vital importance.

● With a partner decide what publications the following reviews appeared in.

Jacko Wows 'em at Wembley!

Wacko Jacko might be weird – but last night he proved to 75,000 adoring fans that he is totally wonderful too.

Wembley Stadium has witnessed some glorious scenes in its time. But it has never seen anything like Michael Jackson, the undisputed king of rock.

Not even Jacko's superstar rivals Bruce Springsteen, Madonna, David Bowie or Prince, could conjure up the sort of frenzy produced by the stage wizard last night.

It left the fans spellbound.

From the moment the singer's slight frame bounded onto the stage and ripped into Wanna Be Startin' Something, you knew that something really was starting. Something wonderful.

FORGET weirdo, wacko, wimpo Jacko. On stage, dressed head to foot in his black punk leathers, the man is pure macho dynamite.

FORGET Michael Jackson the virgin. On stage, with his sensual, gyrating, hip thrusting dances, the man is pure sex.

FORGET Jackson the chartbusting pop star. When you witness Jacko's breathtaking showmanship, you cannot describe Michael as merely a singer.

The man is **PURE** showbiz.

With his astonishing energy – he never stopped moving for his entire two hour, sixteen-song show – Jackson managed to draw on the talents of dancer Fred Astaire, mime master Marcel Marceau and the magic of Harry Houdini.

Jackson didn't waste time on lengthy introductions. He didn't need to. Each number was a classic. **EVERYONE** knew them.

There were modern smash hits like Bad, Dirty Diana, Billy Jean, Thriller and Beat It.

And, much to the delight of the huge floodlit crowd, Michael went right back to his early days when he belted out a Jackson Five Motown Medley including I Want You Back and ABC.

The show was very carefully stage managed. There were elaborate costume changes. At the end of Dirty Diana he darted into a tent at the back of the vast stage and emerged seconds later wearing a werewolf mask for Thriller.

For Smooth Criminal quick change Jacko wore a slick white suit with matching trilby to turn himself into a caricature Chicago gangster.

Sensual

Jackson's sensual stage act reached boiling point when he thrust his snake-like hips suggestively at the luckiest girl in the whole stadium, his stunning blonde singer Shirley Crowe.

And then there was the highlight of the night.

It's difficult to find words to describe what happened during Beat It. But here goes . . .

Now you see him, now you don't. A huge puff of smoke enveloped Michael and the crowd gasped as he simply disappeared!

Seconds later the showman to beat all showmen rematerialised – as if by magic – on the other side of the stage on top of a giant 25 foot gantry wearing a wizard black satin cape.

And if anyone deserved to portray himself as a wizard, it was Mr Michael Jackson.

The crowd loved him, and he loved the crowd.

Everyone, especially Jackson himself, had fun at Wembley.

It made a Cup Final look tame.

The Greatest Showman

Occasionally one wishes one had trained as a ticket tout. Michael Jackson has racked up an implausible seven sell-outs at Wembley Stadium, and it's difficult to believe there could be anybody left on earth wanting tickets. But people were paying upwards of £150 a throw outside, despite a plea from Michael which mysteriously materialised in the press.

"Don't deal with these people," he is believed to have said, though it isn't clear to whom. "They make me so mad." Sometimes, it's possible to believe he may be human.

Perhaps Michael is beginning to draw crowds from distant solar systems, let alone Terence Trent D'Arby and Jack Nicholson, both spotted ducking into VIP boxes. Certainly, the air of unreality was tangible enough to take home in cans.

By the time he kicked off last night with Got To Be Starting Something, the crowd, many of whom had been inside the stadium since the 4.30 pm opening time, had built up a head of restless energy which the star blithely channelled into his performance. Part of the Jackson mystique is his capacity for making 72,000 people willing accomplices in his dream world, however ludicrous or irrational that may be. By the 10.30 close, thousands of lighters were waving aloft as the star shimmered off down the yellow brick road to his hotel.

Viewed with analytic rigour there isn't a lot in Jackson's music to phone home about. If you were to name your 10 favourite songs, I doubt there would be one of his among them, though Man In The Mirror (saved for his final encore) might be a close contender.

But for all his alleged foibles, and weakness for children and small animals, Jackson generates a cruel tension which slices through the bland jazz-funk tendencies of his band. He dances with a taut, stabbing precision which defies his compadres to miss a beat. He embodies perfection, and he makes it look painful.

He's a peerless showman even in a football stadium. Costume changes are manipulated with a magician's slickness, through the ghouls-and-zombies routine of Thriller via a gangland Beat It to a glitzy burst of St Valentine's Day violence, where Michael machine-guns his squad of dancers.

Jackson has dissolved the glue between fact and fiction, burying the human being but selling the familiar sound and screen image with hallucinatory intensity. The live show is like the videos, but more so, and for every dizzying spin and reverse-walk he pulls off in the flesh, the dazzling video image alongside does it 10 times better.

For Thriller, he appeared in a werewolf mask as a huge Thriller filled the video screens, and the crowd bellowed its recognition. When he sang Human Nature, he robot-walked his way through it with no apparent sense of irony. In I Just Can't Stop Loving You, Jackson's painted,

sweat-stained features were thrust out on screen in grotesque close-up.

It's the ultimate Greatest Hit package, blanketing all media simultaneously. Logistically, Jackson's tour resembled a small war working its way round the European continent. Three million European fans will have seen him perform by the end of August, which means a gross box-office take of approximately £60 million. Over 300 tons of equipment is being dragged from the Pyrenees to the Pennines in 11 articulated lorries, and the core of 120 tour personnel is augmented by up to 500 helpers hired locally for each show.

There are the usual megastar spin-offs to offset the aura of incalculable collateral continually mounting. An assortment of charities will benefit from this landslide of Jackomania, including Save The Children, Great Ormond Street Hospital and the Prince's Trust.

The tour has also made stars of Mike's manager, Frank Dileo, and his producer Quincy Jones, both of whom have been given their own individual biogs from the record company.

Maybe it's the greatest show on earth, maybe it's the last time Jackson will tread the boards before he heads for celluloid and the Hollywood Hills. Or maybe not. But you'll be kicking yourself forever if you miss it.

● On a scale of 1–5, how many points would you give each passage for the following qualities of style:

Relaxed	Formal
Informative	Chatty
Critical	Complimentary
Lively	Dull

● Produce three reviews of a recent concert, a concert video or a new album:
a) for a pop magazine,
b) for a tabloid newspaper, and
c) for a serious newspaper.
   Your audiences will be, broadly speaking,
a) fans,
b) sensation seekers,
c) people with a general interest in a wide range of music. You will need to decide what prior information your audience possesses, what you think they'll really want to know and in what style you should write.

SAY IT RIGHT

As we have seen, the way language is used is often dictated by the 'intended audience' of the piece – whether it is written or spoken. The same information or ideas can be communicated in a variety of ways depending on the nature of that audience.

In talking, it is usually very obvious who the intended audience is, and what the relationship is between the deliverer of information and the audience. We are remarkably skilled at judging the relationships between people just from little 'snippets' of talk.

In the following poem, the poet is using two 'voices', each addressing a different audience, each in a different style and delivering a contrasting set of information.

The picture below is one illustrator's interpretation of the poem *Naming of Parts*. What would yours be?

Naming of Parts

Today we have naming of parts. Yesterday,
We had daily cleaning. And tomorrow morning,
We shall have what to do after firing. But today,
Today we have naming of parts. Japonica
Glistens like coral in all of the neighbouring gardens,
And today we have naming of parts.

This is the lower sling swivel. And this
Is the upper sling swivel, whose use you will see,
When you are given your slings. And this is the piling
   swivel,
Which in your case you have not got. The branches
Hold in the gardens their silent, eloquent gestures,
Which in our case we have not got.

This is the safety-catch, which is always released
With an easy flick of the thumb. And please do not let me
See anyone using his finger. You can do it quite easy
If you have any strength in your thumb. The blossoms
Are fragile and motionless, never letting anyone see
Any of them using their finger.

And this you can see is the bolt. The purpose of this
Is to open the breech, as you see. We can slide it
Rapidly backwards and forwards: we call this
Easing the spring. And rapidly backwards and forwards,
The early bees are assaulting and fumbling the flowers:
They call it easing the spring.

They call it easing the spring: it is perfectly easy
If you have any strength in your thumb: like the bolt,
And the breech, and the cocking-piece, and the point of
   balance,
Which in our case we have not got; and the almond-
   blossom
Silent in all of the gardens and the bees going backwards
   and forwards,
For today we have naming of parts.
Henry Reed

Options

● Look closely at this poem, and try to identify the two voices. What effect does the poet achieve by using these contrasting voices?

● Write a similar poem, containing two voices, about yourself. Use a conversational style for your 'first voice', with your chosen audience firmly in mind – you might be addressing a friend, a member of the opposite sex, a teacher. The situation might be a first date, a careers interview, or simply a chat about your future. For your 'second voice', look back at your stream-of-consciousness piece, and pick out lines or ideas that you could use. The 'second voice' in the poem will be your real self – the person whom only you really know – and its intended audience will be you. Combine the two voices in a poem.

Playwrights often give very clear instructions on how particular lines in plays are to be spoken. Why do you think this is done? What extra information does the playwright wish to communicate?

The relationships between the characters in the following prose extract are quite clear – but if this were a play, what information would the author supply in brackets to show how the characters should address each other?

Now Miss Crocker made a startling announcement: this year we would all have books.

Everyone gasped, for most of the students had never handled a book at all besides the family Bible. I admit that even I was somewhat excited. Although Mama had several books, I had never had one of my very own.

"Now we're very fortunate to get these readers," Miss Crocker explained while we eagerly awaited the unveiling. "The county superintendent of schools himself brought these books down here for our use and we must take extra-good care of them." She moved toward her desk. "So let's all promise that we'll take the best care possible of these new books." She stared down, expecting our response. "All right, all together, let's repeat, 'We promise to take good care of our new books.' 'She looked sharply at me as she spoke.

"WE PROMISE TO TAKE GOOD CARE OF OUR NEW BOOKS!"

"Fine," Miss Crocker beamed, then proudly threw back the tarpaulin.

Sitting so close to the desk, I could see that the covers of the books, a motley red, were badly worn and that the grey edges of the pages had been marred by pencils, crayons, and ink. My anticipation at having my own book ebbed to a sinking disappointment. But Miss Crocker continued to beam as she called each fourth grader to her desk and, recording a number in her roll book, handed him or her a book.

As I returned from my trip to her desk, I noticed the first graders anxiously watching the disappearing pile. Miss Crocker must have noticed them too, for as I sat down she said, "Don't worry, little ones, there are plenty of readers for you too. See there on Miss Davis's desk." Wide eyes turned to the covered teacher's platform directly in front of them and an audible sigh of relief swelled in the room.

I glanced across at Little Man, his face lit in eager excitement. I knew that he could not see the soiled covers or the marred pages from where he sat, and even though his penchant for cleanliness was often annoying I did not like to think of his disappointment when he saw the books as they really were. But there was nothing that I could do about it, so I opened my book to its center and began browsing through the spotted pages. Girls with blonde braids and boys with blue eyes stared up at me. I found a story about a boy and his dog lost in a cave and began reading while Miss Crocker's voice droned on monotonously.

Suddenly I grew conscious of a break in that monotonous tone and I looked up. Miss Crocker was sitting at Miss Davis's desk with the first-grade books stacked before her, staring fiercely down at Little Man, who was pushing a book back upon the desk.

"What's that you said, Clayton Chester Logan?" she asked.

The room became gravely silent. Everyone knew that Little Man was in big trouble for no one, but no one, ever called Little Man "Clayton Chester" unless she or he meant serious business.

Little Man knew this too. His lips parted slightly as he took his hands from the book. He quivered, but he did not take his eyes from Miss Crocker. "I—I said may I have another book please, ma'am," he squeaked. "That one's dirty."

"Dirty!" Miss Crocker echoed, appalled by such temerity. She stood up, gazing down upon Little Man like a bony giant, but Little Man raised his head and continued to look into her eyes. "Dirty! And just who do you think you are, Clayton Chester? Here the county is giving us these wonderful books during these hard times and you're going to stand there and tell me that the book's too dirty? Now you take that book or get nothing at all!"

Little Man lowered his eyes and said nothing as he stared at the book. For several moments he stood there, his face barely visible above the desk, then he turned and looked at the few remaining books and, seeming to realize that they were as badly soiled as the one Miss Crocker had given him, he looked across the room at me. I nodded and Little Man, glancing up again at Miss Crocker, slid the book from the edge of the desk, and with his back straight and his head up returned to his seat.

Miss Crocker sat down again. "Some people around here seem to be giving themselves airs. I'll tolerate no more of that," she scowled. "Sharon Lake, come get your book."

I watched Little Man as he scooted into his seat beside two other little boys. He sat for a while with a stony face looking out the window; then, evidently accepting the fact that the book in front of him was the best that he could expect, he turned and opened it. But as he stared at the book's inside cover, his face clouded, changing from sulky acceptance to puzzlement. His brows furrowed. Then his eyes grew wide, and suddenly he sucked in his breath and sprang from his chair like a wounded animal, flinging the book onto the floor and stomping madly upon it.

Miss Crocker rushed to Little Man and grabbed him up in powerful hands. She shook him vigorously, then set him on the floor again. "Now, just what's gotten into you, Clayton Chester?"

But Little Man said nothing. He just stood staring down at the open book, shivering with indignant anger.

"Pick it up," she ordered.

"No!" defied Little Man.

"No? I'll give you ten seconds to pick up that book, boy, or I'm going to get my switch."

Little Man bit his lower lip, and I knew that he was not going to pick up the book. Rapidly, I turned to the inside cover of my own book and saw immediately what had made Little Man so furious. Stamped on the inside cover was a chart which read:

PROPERTY OF THE BOARD OF EDUCATION
Spokane County, Mississippi
September, 1922

CHRONOLOGICAL ISSUANCE	DATE OF ISSUANCE	CONDITION OF BOOK	RACE OF STUDENT
1	September 1922	New	White
2	September 1923	Excellent	White
3	September 1924	Excellent	White
4	September 1925	Very Good	White
5	September 1926	Good	White
6	September 1927	Good	White
7	September 1928	Average	White
8	September 1929	Average	White
9	September 1930	Average	White
10	September 1931	Poor	White
11	September 1932	Poor	White
12	September 1933	Very Poor	nigra
13			
14			
15			
16			

The blank lines continued down to line 20 and I knew that they had all been reserved for black students. A knot of anger swelled in my throat and held there. But as Miss Crocker directed Little Man to bend over the "whipping" chair, I put aside my anger and jumped up.

"Miz Crocker, don't, please!" I cried. Miss Crocker's dark eyes warned me not to say another word. "I know why he done it!"

"You want part of this switch, Cassie?"

"No'm," I said hastily. "I just wanna tell you how come Little Man done what he done."

"Sit down!" she ordered as I hurried towards her with the open book in my hand.

Holding the book up to her, I said, "See, Miz Crocker, see what it says. They give us these ole books when they didn't want 'em no more."

She regarded me impatiently, but did not look at the book. "Now how could he know what it says? He can't read."

"Yes'm, he can. He been reading since he was four. He can't read all them big words, but he can read them columns. See what's in the last row. Please look, Miz Crocker."

This time Miss Crocker did look, but her face did not change. Then holding up her head, she gazed unblinkingly down at me.

"S-see what they called us," I said, afraid she had not seen.

"That's what you are," she said coldly. "Now go sit down."

I shook my head, realising now that Miss Crocker did not even know what I was talking about. She had looked at the page and had understood nothing.

"I said sit down, Cassie!"

I started slowly toward my desk, but as the hickory stick sliced the tense air, I turned back around. "Miz Crocker," I said, "I don't want my book neither."

The switch landed hard upon Little Man's upturned bottom. Miss Crocker looked questioningly at me as I reached up to her desk and placed the book upon it. Then she swung the switch five more times and, discovering that Little Man had no intention of crying, ordered him up.

"All right, Cassie," she sighed, turning to me, "come on and get yours."

Mildred Taylor, *Roll of Thunder, Hear My Cry*

Options

● Try rewriting the piece as a drama script, using the dialogue as it appears in the extract, but adding stage directions to show how the lines should be spoken – the prose extract itself should give you all the information you need. You could even extend the story if you wish.

● The extract has been written in the first person: we get the impression that Cassie is confiding in us. But if she were addressing someone else, through a different form of writing, how might the expression of her feelings change? Using only the information given in the passage, write one or all of the following pieces:
a) a letter written by Cassie to the Chairman of the Board of Education, protesting against the situation.
b) a piece of poetry which Cassie intends to show to no one else.
c) an article written by Cassie twenty years later, and addressed to the readers of a newspaper.

● Explore any poetry anthology for poems that are concerned with the expression of feelings related to personal experiences. Use one of these poems as the basis for pieces of writing similar to those above.

● You will find pairs of roleplay cards on *Repromaster 31*. Working in pairs, each take a card. Do not show it to your partner. Using the information on it, write a short piece about how your character *really* feels. Then, in your pairs, perform the role play. When you have finished, try to work out what the *other* character's feelings were. (You might like to write this down.) Check against your partner's piece of writing to see how close you came.

KEEPING IT SIMPLE

Keeping It Simple

Technical or specialist language is a style of language that we gradually grow into. The process becomes a serious business when we have to learn the vocabulary that is used, for example, in science, geography and mathematics lessons. It can be a long, slow process.

*The following example of technical writing, produced by a ten-year-old (from the **Complete Plain Words** by Sir Ernest Gowers) shows the very basic honesty and simplicity with which we tend to write when we are very young.*

The bird that I am going to write about is the owl. The owl cannot see at all by day and at night is as blind as a bat.

I do not know much about the owl, so I will go on to the beast which I am going to choose. It is the cow. The cow is a mammal. It has six sides – right, left, an upper and below. At the back it has a tail on which hangs a brush. With this it sends the flies away so that they do not fall into the milk. The head is for the purpose of growing horns and so that the mouth can be somewhere. The horns are to butt with, and the mouth is to moo with. Under the cow hangs the milk. It is arranged for milking. When people milk, the milk comes and there is never an end to the supply. How the cow does it I have not yet realised, but it makes more and more. The cow has a fine sense of smell; one can smell it far away. This is the reason for the fresh air in the country.

The man cow is called an ox. It is not a mammal. The cow does not eat much, but what it eats it eats twice, so that it gets enough. When it is hungry it moos, and when it says nothing it is because its inside is all full up with grass.

As an adult the same person may be as guilty as many others of producing practically unreadable pieces of writing. If this young author were to end up working for an insurance company as an adult, he or she might eventually be asked to write something like this:

Public Liability

To indemnify the insured in respect of legal liability to the public for injury to persons (not a member of the insured's family or household) and/or damage to property (excluding the insured's own or that of members of his family or household) up to a limit of £250,000 any one accident or series of accidents and in all (including legal expenses) arising from accidents occurring in connection with the trip during the period of the insurance, but excluding liabilities arising out of the ownership or use of any horse drawn or mechanically propelled vehicle, waterborne craft or aircraft, lands, buildings and excluding professional and contractual liability and liability to employees. No liability shall be admitted and no admission, arrangement, offer, promise or payment shall be made by the insured without the written consent of underwriters, who shall be entitled, if they so desire, to take over and conduct in the name of the insured their defence of any claim or to prosecute in his (their) name for their own benefit any claims for indemnity or damages or otherwise against any third party, and shall have full discretion in the conduct of any negotiations or proceedings or the settlement of any claim, and the insured shall, whenever possible, give all such information and assistance as underwriters may require.

● The language of official documents often causes great difficulty for those trying to understand it. Try and unscramble the following, slightly easier example, rewriting it in a simpler way.

If the insured person(s) has/have not completed his/her/their travel before the expiration of this insurance for reasons which are beyond his/her/their control this insurance will remain in force until completion not exceeding a further 21 days without additional premium, but in the event of an insured person being hi-jacked cover shall continue whilst the insured person is subject to the control of the person(s) or their associates making the hi-jack and during travel direct to his domicile and/or original destination for a period not exceeding twelve months from the date of the hi-jack.

Many official bodies have recently made great efforts to improve their forms and pamphlets. The process itself is not easy.

To write a simple form, the Plain English Society offers the following guidelines:

1. Decide the purpose of the information you are going to give.
2. Build up a picture of your readers. (Age? Occupation? What newspapers do they read?)
3. Decide on what is essential information and stick to it.
4. Think carefully about how to present the information. (Questions? Checklist? Charts/diagrams?)
5. Organise the information in a logical order. ('First do this . . .' etc.)
6. Get the beginning right (capture the reader's attention straight away).
7. Imagine the reader knows practically nothing about the subject.
8. Write as if explaining the points to a group of typical readers in the room with you.
9. Try to sell the information (almost like an advertisement – but not 'over the top').
10. Construct simple sentences that are less than twenty words in length (sometimes much shorter – for effect).
11. Choose words learnt easily in life.
12. Leave plenty of areas of white space.
13. Make sure the type is big enough for your intended readers.
14. Make sure the overall effect is pleasing to the eye.

Finally they recommend that you test the level of difficulty by using a 'readability test'.

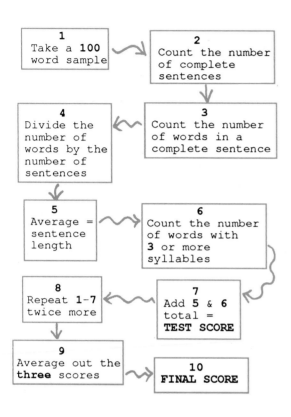

| 1 Take a **100** word sample |
| 2 Count the number of complete sentences |
| 3 Count the number of words in a complete sentence |
| 4 Divide the number of words by the number of sentences |
| 5 Average = sentence length |
| 6 Count the number of words with **3** or more syllables |
| 7 Add **5** & **6** total = **TEST SCORE** |
| 8 Repeat **1-7** twice more |
| 9 Average out the **three** scores |
| 10 **FINAL SCORE** |

The National Consumer Council worked out the following scores for newspapers in 1980. The lower the score, the easier the material is to understand.

The Sun	26
Daily Mirror	28
Daily Express	29
Daily Mail	31
Morning Star	34
Daily Telegraph	34
The Times	36
The Guardian	39

Options

● Try out the readability test yourselves on newspapers. You must use the same type of article when making comparisons between different newspapers – news reports are the best.

● Produce a simple application form for a pen-pal club. You will need to make sure that the form, when completed, will contain as much useful information as possible, so that every applicant has a good chance of finding a suitable pen-pal.

● Produce an official application form that could be used in school – Fourth Year options may be a good area to examine. Use the checklist of fourteen points during the preparation of the form. As a class, you may need to interview subject teachers in order to obtain relevant information that you can use in brief paragraphs about each subject on offer. Or you might just wish to design an options application form that collects information relevant to a pupil's career ambitions.

● Examine the form below. How well have the fourteen points been considered in the design of the form? Do a readability test on the form. Produce a simplified version of this form or of one of your choice. Write a letter explaining the ways in which your revised form differs from the original – you might attempt to 'sell' your simplified and improved version to the insurance company which produced the original.

VARIATIONS

Horror Film

Well sir, first of all there was this monster
But like he's not really a monster
'Cause in real life he's a bank clerk sir
And sings in this village choir
But he keeps like drinking this potion sir
And you see him like changing into this pig
With black curly hairs on its knuckles;
And what he does sir,
Is he goes round eating people's brains.
Anyway before that sir, I should have said
He's secretly in love with Lady Irene
Who's very rich with lots of long frocks
And she has this identical twin sister
Who looks like her sir
Who keeps getting chased by this monster bulldog
Into these sinking sands
That's inhabited by this prehistoric squid sir
Which like she can't see
Because the deaf and dumb bailiff
With the hump on his back
Has trod on her specs.
Anyway before that sir,
I should have said,
This lady Irene is screaming,
'Henry, Henry, my beloved, save me,'
'Cause she's been walled up in the dripping dungeon
With the mad violinist of the vaults
By the manservant with the withered boot sir.
But this Henry, he can't hear her sir,
Because he's too busy
Putting people in this bubbling acid bath
To make them stay young forever sir
But his experiments keep going wrong.
Anyway, before that sir,
I should have said,
Her Dad can't rescue her either sir
Because of the army of giant ants
That's eating his castle;
And the music sir, it's going,
'Tarrar, tarrar, boom boom tarrar sir,'
And 'Henry, Henry my beloved,'
She keeps screaming
And the mad violinist of the vaults sir
He starts going funny all over the flagstones.
And like, Algernon sir,
No not him sir, the other one,
He can't do nothing about the squid in the bogs
Because he's turning into this pig with hairy knuckles.
Anyway before that sir, I should have said,
There's this huge mummy in the library
And every time he hears this music
Starts tearing off all these dirty bandages
And smashing through these walls and everything
And the professor can't stop him

'Cause he's gone off his rocker
And keeps bulging his eyes and laughing a lot
When suddenly this vampire . . .
Didn't I tell you about the vampire sir?
Anyway before that there's this vampire
Who's been dead for thousands of years
But he's a Swiss greengrocer in real life
But the iceberg his coffin's in
Gets all broken up sir
When it collides with Dr Strenkhoff's submarine sir,
That's carrying this secret cargo
Of radio active rats . . .
Didn't I tell you about the radio active rats sir?
Well anyway sir
Before that I should have said . . .
Gareth Owen

A Word in Edgeways

Tell me about yourself they
say and you begin to
tell them about yourself and
that is just the way I
am is their reply: they play
it all back to you in another
key, their key, and then in mid-
narrative they pay you a
compliment as if to say what a good
listener you are I am
a good listener my stay
here has developed my faculty I will
say that for me I will not
say that every literate male in
America is a soliloquist, a
ventriloquist, a strategic
egotist, an inveterate
campaigner-explainer over and
back again on the terrain of himself – what I will
say is they are not un-
interesting: they are simply
unreciprocal and yes it was a
pleasure if not an unmitigated
pleasure and I yes I did enjoy our
conversation goodnightthankyou
Charles Tomlinson

But he didn't have time to eat it.
As he got nearer, he could hear a
munching noise. His breakfast was
being eaten by something.
In a few seconds, his breakfast
was gone !!!

Martin Waddell on Writing

"It helps you to understand yourself, because in everything you write, you do in fact confront yourself – you confront bits of your mind which you didn't know about. You suddenly find that a bit of your mind knows about a whole area of experience, and it's interesting to go into that and find out what you know and what you feel. I write many children's stories, which are close to fable in some cases, and in that process, a tremendous amount of exploration goes on.

"You get people saying, 'I could write a book,' and what they're talking about is the fact that they once went to Egypt and met a man who'd met Colonel Nasser – and what they don't look at is their own backyard, because in their own backyard there *is* a book. I think it's when you begin to look at your own entrails that you find that there's all sorts of things there, and the technique of writing is learning to spin those things. But the actual material is there; it's whether you can tap into that material."

ACCENTUATE THE POSITIVE

ACCENTS & DIALECTS

Everyone speaks with an accent that varies depending upon the area in which they live, the social group to which they belong and the education which they receive. To put it simply, accent is the way we pronounce our words. Social groups are important in dictating the form which accents take. The location and type of school we attend is also important, because the greatest influence on the way we talk as young people is the young people we talk with all day and every day.

● Listen to the young people on the tape discussing accent and dialect.

In addition, we all talk in a dialect. An easy way to remember the difference between accent and dialect is to remember that an accent is simply the way we pronounce our words, whilst a dialect has its own particular words and phrases, as well as its own style of pronunciation.

If it surprises you to think that you speak a dialect, look through the following list – say them out loud to yourself. How many of these phrases sound right to you?

I done it.
He want them.
You seen her.
Them people are foolish.
You had a good time, hadn't you?
There isn't no sweets for you.
I don't want none.
It wasn't no good.
My brother he's playing upstairs.
I ain't done it.
She's hardworking is Sarah.
Zoë and Ben is going to school.
I give him a present yesterday.
She was sat over here.
It's more than ten mile away.
You need two pound for a ticket.
The room is twelve foot wide.
Did you listen to that record yet?
You haven't got to forget your homework.
He knocked his drink off of the table.
Look at them cars over there.
You should of done that by now.
The woman what said it.
Them ones over there.
She weren't here.
They wasn't ready.
No, I never did that.
I won't do nothing.
She said that, I never.
You shouldna done that.
She like sweets.
He's daft, him.
There's eggs in that bag.

I does it at school.
He was stood over there.
Don't be talking like that.
Look at this here book.
Give it me, it's mine.
He likes that hisself.
Do it, else I'll go crazy.
I'm going down my friend's house.
These are the records what I like best.
I've got a old hi-fi.

Some of these phrases will sound right to you as they will be common to your local dialect. None of them is incorrect, because they do not break the rules, since every dialect of the English language has its own set of rules. On the other hand each and every one of them breaks the rules of the Standard English dialect. It is for this reason and this reason alone that your parents will correct such 'mistakes' in your speech, and probably your teachers will correct such 'mistakes' in your writing. The chances are, though, that in a relaxed situation (talking with your friends, for example) you will continue to use your natural dialect. It is because people feel pressurised to adopt a dialect which is not natural to them that many people feel slightly ashamed of the way they talk. Peter Trudgill, a Professor of Language, has this to say:

If you tell a child often enough that his dialect is 'wrong' you will not succeed in getting him to change it, but you almost certainly will succeed in making him very unsure about his language. He will not be encouraged to speak a new dialect. He will simply be discouraged from speaking at all. Years of the 'elimination' approach have not succeeded in doing any eliminating. But they have, unfortunately, succeeded in convincing a majority of the nation's inhabitants that they 'can't speak English'.

When I was making a study of the way English is spoken in Norwich, at least half of the people I spoke to and tape-recorded expressed surprise that I should want to talk to them. They would say things like "I'm a very poor talker"; "I know I speak horrible"; "I can't speak English properly". This was particularly sad because most of them then proceeded to give a very convincing demonstration of the fact that they could speak English not only fluently (which is only what one would expect from a native speaker after all) but also vividly, clearly, entertainingly and in a highly skilful manner. (There is nothing unusual about Norwich people in this, of course. My experience has been shared by many others in other parts of the country.)

If many people hold views like this about the value of their own dialects, it is not surprising if some of them, both adults and children, become hesitant and inarticulate when required to speak in certain circumstances. They are reluctant to say anything lest they reveal their 'inability' to speak the language. We can probably agree that one of the tasks of the school is to give children confidence in their ability to use language. This they will not have if they are required to direct half their attention to how they are saying things – in case they make a 'mistake' – rather than to what they are saying.

Peter Trudgill, *Accent, Dialect and the School*

Options

● With a partner, list the occasions on which you have felt under pressure to speak correctly – the visit of an elderly relative, meeting your boyfriend's or girlfriend's parents for the first time, or making an important telephone call. Who put you under pressure, and how did you feel as a result? Was anyone openly critical of you? Did you conform to the expectations of others and attempt to change the way you speak? Did you simply 'clam up'?

● Roleplay with your partner one of the situations you have just listed. This time you might like to play the part of the person criticising, or you might like to re-enact the scene playing yourself – but this time try to react differently to any pressure put on you.

● Interview a number of people in the community, asking them what they feel about the way they talk. Write up your findings in a report.

● Listen carefully to a radio station playing popular music (Radio One, local radio stations) and pick out phrases used by the presenters that break the rules of Standard English. Write a letter, as yourself, a parent or an English teacher, complaining about the 'bad example set for the young people of today'. Then write a reply from the producer of the programme.

Perhaps the time when someone feels most insecure about the way they talk is when they move from one part of the country to another. Have a look at the following account.

Speech Communities

I moved to London with my family about six years ago. At that time I had a strong Yorkshire accent and soon found that it led me into many difficulties with the London school children. I developed a second accent and now use one in London and my 'old' one when I am in Yorkshire.

Moving to London caused lots of problems. I had trouble in making friends and I eventually put it down to my dialect. It prevented people from understanding what I was saying, so I stopped using it. This, of course, was difficult, because by that time it had become a habit. Children still chose not to be my friend. My speech had shown them I was a complete outsider and they were to have nothing to do with me. Some of the words I used were 'spice' meaning sweets, 'tha' (thou) meaning you, and 't', which is an abbreviation for the, and is used nearly all the time. However, I was not accepted. Over the years I have suffered much criticism because of my speech.

I was a country bumpkin, and therefore thick, slow and stupid. A recent one was "You northerner!" which was usually followed by a lecture on how northerners were

unfashionable and still listened to the Bay City Rollers. All the children went through my origins. "Are you Scottish or Irish?" According to them everyone from the north of England was either Scottish or Irish. Hence the assumption that as a northerner I still admired the Bay City Rollers.

This, I now realise, is all very trivial, although in some way I regretted my dialect and the bad fortune of having it. This attitude was brought about through all the hatred I received. The pressure from the other children was unfair but it was wrong for me to have to feel ashamed of myself.

This is the attitude brought about in communities. They build up an invisible wall around themselves and no one is allowed in. They exclude any 'differences' from their activities. This makes them very patronising towards the one person who is a long way from his or her own community.

I do not feel that there are many bad points to an accent and dialect, so what I have shown are the difficulties that face a person when entering a new group of people.

I am pleased with being able to have two accents and dialects and think that, considering my situation, I have nonetheless done quite well!

Madeleine Rock

● With a partner, list all the problems that the writer has faced because of her accent and dialect.

● Work out a sentence that describes her feelings about her experience.

● Use the sentence you have devised as the title for your own story about the prejudices suffered by someone, because of the way they talk, when moving into a new area.

Social and professional groupings can have a great influence on accent and dialect, but this isn't always the case; for instance, though schoolteachers from Birmingham and Yorkshire might speak in roughly the same dialect, farmers from the same two areas might talk very differently.

JUDGING BY ...

''It is impossible for an Englishman to open his mouth, without making some other Englishman despise him.''
George Bernard Shaw

Most people in Britain have very definite preferences when it comes to regional accents, and many are disliked.

● Listen to the examples of regional accents on the tape. As you are doing so:
a) Note down where you think the accent originates from (use the map on *Repromaster 33* to indicate the origin of each).
b) Write down one word to describe the accent.

● Now put your list of accents in order of preference. Make a class chart of the accents (10 points if it came tenth on someone's list and so on – the one with least points will come out top). Then build up a picture of the accents using the individual words each member of the class used to describe them. Discuss your final list. What conclusions do you draw from the class' reactions? In what situations might those people with accents at the bottom of your list suffer? Is it reasonable that people should suffer because of their accents?

Every part of the British Isles has its own accent and dialect, but one accent in particular has become associated with 'proper English': Received Pronunciation, or RP. Geographically, it is associated with London and South-East England; but because London is the political and commercial capital of Britain, RP has also become associated with power, wealth and status. Academics have divided RP itself into two classes: 'unmarked' RP (spoken by many television newsreaders) and 'marked' RP ('posh English', as spoken by certain members of the royal family). A Scottish equivalent of English RP is the Morningside Edinburgh accent.

The following extract, from a book entitled **The Queen's English – High Taw Tawk Prawpah-Leah,** *makes fun of 'marked' RP. Decide for yourself how exaggerated it is!*

Goldilocks and the Three Bears

Once upon a time, there was a little girl and her name was Goldilocks. One day, as she ran in the woods, she came across a pretty cottage. The door of the cottage was open and she decided to go inside and have a look round. What a naughty girl she was! She entered and spied a table already set for breakfast, with three plates of porridge upon it.

Goldilocks sat down and started to eat from the biggest plate of porridge.

''This porridge is too hot and too lumpy,'' she said to herself.

So saying, she sat down in front of the middle-sized plate and commenced to eat that.

''This porridge is too cold and too salty,'' she cried.

Goldilocks then sat down before the smallest plate, picked up the spoon and had a mouthful.

''This porridge is just right,'' she exclaimed happily, and she proceeded to eat it all up.

When she had finished, she was very tired and climbed the stairs in order to have a rest.

Upstairs she found three beds. There was a large bed, a middle-sized bed and a little baby bed. Goldilocks lay down on the big bed first.

''This bed is too hard,'' she cried, and tried the middle-sized bed.

''This bed is too soft,'' she expostulated, and moved on to the little baby bed. She lay down on it and smiled, for she was surprised.

''This baby bed is just right,'' she shouted loudly, and in no time she fell fast asleep.

Just then, the three bears, who were the real owners of the cottage, returned home from an early morning constitutional in the forest. They were aghast at what they found.

''Who's been eating my porridge?'' yelled Daddy Bear.

''Someone's been eating my porridge too,'' said Mummy Bear in amazement.

''Someone's been eating my porridge too,'' cried little baby bear, ''and they've eaten it all up.'' A tear ran down his face.

''We'll see about this,'' said Daddy Bear, racing for the stairs. ''The intruder may still be in our house. Come on!'' he shouted, and ran up the stairs, followed by his wife and child.

They made such a din that Goldilocks heard them and woke up. She ran over to the window, jumped out and dashed off into the bushes, weeping and crying.

Goldilocks never went into the woods again, but stayed close to her Mummy and her Daddy, and lived happily ever after.

The End.

Galed-ear-lawks end theh Threah Bahs

Worns ay pornay tame, thah wores ay lear-till ghel end hah neem wores Galed-ear-lawks. Worn dear, ears sheer ren Ian thah wards, sheer kem earcraws ay pree-teah caught-itch. Thah daw awv thah caught-itch wores air-pin end sheer dear-sayed-dead taw gay Ian-sayed end hevvah lawk rind. Wart ay knot-ear ghel sheer wores! Shen-tarred end spayed ay teable awl rid-ear sit faw Brie-ache-fawst, weirth threa pleats awv poor-itch ay-porn eat.

Galed-ear-lawks set dine end stawtid taw ate frawm thah beer-ghist pleat awv poor-itch.

"These poor-itch ease taw hawt end taw lahm-pear," sheer sid taw hah-sylph.

Sue seeing, sheer set dine Ian frahn-tawv theh meed-ill saisd pleat end caw-minced taw ate thet.

"These poor-itch ease taw kaled end taw saul-tear," sheer krayed.

Galed-ear-lawks thin set dine beefah theh smol-est pleat, peaked ahp theh spawn end hed ay mythe-fall.

"These poor-itch ease jars treat," sheer eeks-clearmd hair-pully, end sheer pru-see-dead taw it eat awl ahp.

Win sheer hed fear-nearshd, sheer wores vireh tayed end claimed theh stars Ian awdah tev ay wrist.

Ahp stars sheer fained threah bids. Thah wores ay lawj bid, ay meed-ill saised bid end ay leetle bear-beer bid. Galed-ear-lawks lee dine awn thah beeg bid fast.

"These bid ease taw whored," sheer krayed, end trayed theh meed-ill saisd bid.

"These bid ease taw sawft," sheer acks-pause-tior-litred, end wint Ava taw theh leetle bear-beer bid. Sheer lee dine awn eat end smaled, fah sheer wores sah-praised.

"These bear-beer bid ease jars treat," sheer shited lied-leh, end eno tame sheer fill faw-store slip.

Jarst thin, that threah bahs, whore wear theh rill anus awv theh caught-itch, ree-tahned frawn in ahlay more-kneeing cawn-steet-yaw-shone-ill Ian theh faw-wrist. Thee worry-gawsed et wart thee fained.

"Whores bin itting may poor-itch?" yeild deadie bah.

"Psalm-worns bin itting may poor-itch taw," sid mah-meah bah Ian arm-airs-mint.

"Psalm-worns bin itting may poor-itch taw," krayed leetle bear-beer bah, "end thev ittin eat awl ahp." Ay T.R. ren dine he's fees.

"Will seer ay-bite these," said deadie bah, reecing farther stars. "Tharn-traw-door me steal beer Ian ah hice. Calm awn!" here shited, end wren ahp theh stars, fall-laid bay he's waif end jailed.

Thee med saachi dean thet Galed-ear-lawks hard thim end woe-carp. Sheer ren Ava taw theh wheen-day, jarmt ite end deshed awf Ian-taw theh borschs, whipping end kraying.

Galed-ear-lawks nivver wint bek Ian taw thah wards ay gayne, bart steed clues taw hah mah-meah end hah deadie, end leaved hair-pully ivvah awftah.

Thinned.

Researchers have shown that, in certain circumstances, an RP accent can be a distinct advantage because of its association with power and authority; but it's not a good idea to adopt it for that reason alone, because RP is also associated with snobbery and privilege, and can have an alienating effect. However, the chances are that you will change your accent, even if only slightly, during your lifetime – though not necessarily to RP. Many people subconsciously pick up the accents of those around them: it's all part of the process of gaining acceptance among friends and colleagues. A move away from your home town – for further education, or to find work – will bring you into contact with other accents, which will influence your own. It is true that the communications revolution of the Twentieth Century – the coming of the telephone, radio and television – has had a powerful effect on regional dialects, many of which are dying out; but accents are still going strong, and are increasingly heard on television – on regional news programmes, on chat shows, and in soap operas.

● How would your accent look, written down? With a partner, try to write a short piece of prose (you could compose a letter to your local paper enthusiastically calling for the preservation of local accents) spelling the words as they sound, to assist pronunciation. You might even decide to really exaggerate your local accent as the 'Goldilocks' extract has done.

It's true to say that people deliberately change their accents from day to day depending upon whom they are talking to. Sometimes this is an attempt to fit in with the crowd, and sometimes there is a social pressure to 'talk properly'.

Options

● Do you believe snobbery exists as far as accents are concerned? Does dislike of particular accents betray a fear or dislike of certain groups in society? Can you think of situations in which people might be looked down upon because of the accent they use? Discuss these points as a class.

● With a partner, roleplay one of the situations the class has just come up with. Then reverse the situation, with the 'dominant' person using an 'inferior' accent, and vice versa.

● Do you think that someone from abroad would make the same kinds of judgements that many British people make about 'posh' or 'common' accents and regional dialects? Why/why not?

SLANGUAGE

Some of the most colourful and lively words and expressions in the language come from slang. Slang, however, is one particular item in the English language that attracts a lot of criticism. We might not think twice about words like 'mob' and 'bully' but in the eighteenth century Jonathan Swift was creating a great fuss about those two particular slang words. Slang is used by all of us, but particularly notable users have been cockneys, cowboys, butchers, young school children and soldiers – to name but a few.

Options

● What do you think about these definitions: "Slang is a language that rolls up its sleeves, spits on its hands and goes to work." "Slang is a poor man's poetry." "The language of slang is the conversation of fools." Which do you prefer? Try to work out your own definition in your group.

● How many slang words can you think of between you that your teacher doesn't know?

● How many can your teacher think of that you don't know?

It should be clear from your discussion and from reading the passage below that while some slang words soon die out, others stay with us.

The Old Santa Fe Trail by **John Young-Hunter**

One of the richest sources of vital new slang has been and still is – the United States. Even more remarkable is the extent to which 19th-century American slang, hated and despised by the English, has now become part of our shared linguistic currency. The pioneers of the Wild West were the fur trappers in the Rockies, the riverboat men of the Mississippi, the Forty-niners in California, the railroad workers on the Union Pacific and the cowboys on the Chisholm trail. A surprising number of everyday English phrases are directly attributable to their experiences.

Out West, the fur trappers gave English 'work like a beaver' and, because they used buckskins as currency, a 'buck' for a dollar. On the Mississippi, a riverboat gambler might 'call your bluff', 'throw in his hand', 'cash in his chips', 'hit the jackpot', 'play a wild card', or even 'pass the buck' – here the buck was the buckhorn-handled knife placed in front of the dealer and passed by a player who did not fancy being in the hot seat – a piece of later gangster slang for the electric chair.

Once the Gold Rush, one of the most remarkable crazes ever to sweep the craze-prone United States, started in 1849, hundreds of thousands of Easterners hurried out West – 'to stake a claim'. They were, of course, hoping for a 'bonanza' (a Spanish word meaning fair weather), or, as they put it, 'a pocket full of rocks'. In California, they would hope that things would 'pan out' (the gold was panned in the rivers), or, if they were mining the ore, that they might 'hit pay dirt' and 'strike it rich'.

The Gold Rush was a freak, and largely an Easterners' experience. The cowboy was the true Westerner or, as some said, 'the real McCoy'. Perhaps the legend of the American cowboy began in the spring of 1867, when the railroad reached Abilene, Kansas. It was here that the young Joseph McCoy had the brainwave that put millions into his bank account and his name into the lexicon. His plan was simple: he would bring the cows up from Texas to the Abilene railhead and ship them back East to feed the big cities. Offering ten times the going rate, he cornered the market. He had boasted that he would deliver 200,000 cattle in ten years. He was wrong. In the first four years alone, he shipped more than two million steers. His performance matched his advertising. He was 'the real McCoy'.

The railroad exported cowboy language back East as well, and so vividly that a New York dentist, Zane Grey, could create a bestselling picture of cowboy society without ever leaving his native city. 'Hot under the collar', 'bite the dust', 'long time no see' and 'no can do' all owe their origins to cowboy and Indian life. The railroad itself, like all powerful new technologies, threw up a swatch of brand-new slang. On its journey, a train might be 'in the clear', or 'have the right of way'. Going uphill, it would 'make the grade' (if it wasn't 'side-tracked'), and finally, having 'let off steam', it would 'reach the end of the line' – assuming it didn't 'go off the rails'.

It is well established that phrases like 'nitty gritty' and 'jam session' come, via pidgin English, from the languages of West Africa. Perhaps less well known is the way in which some of our most fashionable slang came from the jazz parlours of Harlem in the Twenties. One of the high priests of jive talk (as it was known) was Cab Calloway, whose song *Mr Hepster's Jive Talk Dictionary* begins "What's a hepcat? A hepcat is a guy/Who knows all the answers and I'm telling you why . . ." From 'hepcat', we get the slang 'hip', meaning sophisticated – or 'cool' (another Black English expression). In 1938, Calloway published a list of hip words which included several (then quite obscure) slang terms later adopted by millions during the swinging Sixties: 'beat' (exhausted), 'chick'

(girl), 'groovy' (fine), 'hype' (persuasive talk), 'jam' (improvisation), 'riff' (musical phrases), and 'square' (an unhip person).

The black slang of the big city American ghettos is still crossing the Atlantic and being imitated in British playgrounds. Two years ago, the break-dancers and street rappers of North Philadelphia were coining words and phrases that are now commonplace in England: 'fresh' (good); 'fierce' (outstanding); 'bad' (good); 'funky fresh' (very good); 'chill out' (relax); 'house' (to challenge); 'maxing' (chilling out); 'check it out' (watch/listen) and 'jonesing' (wanting something badly). Contemporary white America continues to enrich the language, too. In California, the engine-room of contemporary language change, some 700 new words have been traced to Silicon Valley alone. 'Input', 'interface' and 'software' are no longer state of the art. There's also 'low res' (not too sharp), 'high res' (on the ball), 'interrupt-driven' (frantic), 'core-dumping' (spilling the beans), 'bulkloading' (getting information on board) and 'emulation mode' (ripping off).

While some of this is sure to stick, American jargon can send cold shudders down the English linguistic spine: for the White House spokesman, a parachute drop becomes 'a pre-dawn vertical insertion', and the dead (in Vietnam) are 'inoperative combat personnel'. The US space agency, Nasa, is perhaps the worst offender: at Cape Canaveral you don't say 'Yes', you say 'Affirmative'; when you're safe, you're in a 'benign environment', when the door is shut you have 'latch integrity', when things get dangerous, you're in a 'dynamic environment', and to go to the lavatory you use 'the waste management facility'.
Robert McCrum, *The Listener*, 9 October 1986

Options

● With your group, discuss whether or not the writer considers slang a poor way of talking. Collect phrases from the passage as evidence, and make a list. List the examples of slang that you think the writer dislikes. Do you agree with his verdict? Are there other examples of slang that you object to?

● Give this passage a title that covers the subject and the author's point of view.

Panning for gold

Rhyming slang is to be found in Australia, America and several parts of Britain, but is most commonly associated with the East End of London. The rhymes show a great love of fun and express an enjoyment in playing with language. There was originally a kind of secret society behind its invention, but much of the secrecy has worn off, and you'll probably know some of these: Barnet fair (hair), butcher's hook (look), currant bun (sun), tea leaf (thief), loaf of bread (head), apples and pears (stairs), boat race (face), daisy roots (boots), plates of meat (feet).

● Invent a rhyming dictionary for school – include school subjects, areas of the building, playing truant, school uniform and so on. For example, headmaster – 'sticking plaster', school dinner – 'Derby winner', school bell – 'death knell'.

Another secret type of slang is 'Backslang', used for many years by butchers and some greengrocers (ask your local butcher!). In its original form it simply means 'to speak every word backwards'. You may have used a type of backslang yourself when you were younger – where you move the final sound in the word to the beginning: "a tullit itbe ikel isthe". Or possibly like this – where the first letter, or two letters (if neither are vowels) are placed at the end of the word and the letters 'ay' then added: "isthay is a ittlelay oremay ickytray." This is sometimes known as 'Pig Latin'. 'Arague Language', discovered in places as far apart as Manchester and Chelmsford, goes like this:

Taragoo baraged, saragays slarageepy haragead,
Taragarry ara wharagile, saragays slaragow,
Paragut aragon tharage paragot, saragays grarageedy garagut,
Waragell saragup baragefaragore warage garago.

To bed, says sleepy head,
Tarry a while, says slow,
Put on the pot, says greedy gut,
We'll sup before we go.

Funnily enough, this secret slang was invented in the Nineteenth Century by adults who didn't want their children "tothegee unthegee derthegee standthegee whatthegee theythegee werethegee talkthegee ingthegee abthegee outthegee" (get it?).

Options

● Invent your own set of rules for a secret childhood slang and write a short adventure of a childhood gang in which the slang features. Don't over-use the slang, though, or your story might become unreadable!

● As a class, compile a selection of up-to-the-minute slang words connected with a variety of different subject areas. One group might choose music, another fashion, another sport, and so on.

NO DIALECTS PLEASE!

Apart from the fact that you might not understand this next piece of writing, what else do you notice about it?

Roleplay and improvisation be the two mainstays of modern drama lessons. More complex methodology, what us calls simulation, involves considerable pre-planning. When people speaks of improvisation they be generally alluding to the spontaneous enactment of an idea what has been suggested by the teacher. Roleplay often involves the use of 'role cards', defining the task what is to be completed and a brief description of the characters what are taking part. What us calls simulations often consist of a wide range of interactions around a given situation.

This is a piece of writing you might find in an educational textbook for teachers – but instead of being written in Standard English dialect (the dialect you hear most of the time on television news bulletins and probably from your own teachers) this is written in a West Country dialect. The way that it is written is unusual, but not incorrect. Although Standard English dialect is usually seen to be the true English language, technically there is no such thing as a good dialect and a bad dialect.

● In your groups, discuss your feelings about dialect in general. Are there some dialects you prefer to others? Why? Is dialect:

   a) an important part of your personality?
   b) an entertaining way of talking?
   c) a comfortable way of talking when you are at home?
   d) a comfortable way of talking to friends?
   e) something to be proud of?
   f) something that makes you feel that you belong?
   g) something that makes you feel embarrassed?
   h) an incorrect way of talking?
   i) an old-fashioned way of talking?
   j) a way of talking that should be allowed to die out?
   k) a way of talking that should be encouraged?

Remember: don't confuse accent with dialect. Dialects have their own special words – accent is the way we pronounce the same ordinary words, depending on where we come from.

Is it fair that people are criticised or made fun of for talking in dialect? Kenneth Wadsworth, a Yorkshireman, has this to say about the joy of writing in dialect:

Language is luvly, an dialect words
give colour an warmth to iv'ryday clo'es,
trippin and troopin they fall from mi tongue
an then ah can 'ammer em all into verse.
'Appen ah'm common, but you've no idea
o' t'work and t'pleasure o' summat to say.

Writing about his youth, he has a much less happy story to tell:

Talkin' Brooad

When ah were still nobbut a bairn
an were tekken along to t'schooil
t'teacher shewk 'er 'ead
med me feel a gurt fooil.
Shoo axed me wheear ah lived
an ah said, Oh just up t'rooad . . .
Well, it's kinda 'omely like
is   talkin' brooad.

Soa then she tewk me i' 'and
to learn me things, an by gosh
she sooin med me unnderstand
'at proper fowk talk posh.
It seeams they sa 'better' fer butter
an haitches you cannot afford
to drop – unless you're reight common
an   talkin' brooad.

Soa ah sooin learned to put on an act
an talk wi a plum i' mi mahth,
when t'teacher were theear ah showed tact
an sahnded like sumbdy dahn sahth.
But as sooin as she'd gooan ah stopped
an dropt it just like a gurt looad,
ah'd reyther, until ah get copt,
be   talkin' brooad.

Kenneth Wadsworth

Options

● It is said that when you criticise the way someone talks, you are criticising them deeply. Can you see evidence in the poem that shows how the poet felt and how he reacted? Write a letter as the poet, to the teacher, explaining his feelings as he looks back on the days described in the poem.

● Dialects are often used in drama to create humorous situations. It is the 'inappropriateness' of the language that causes the comic effect. Roleplay a situation in a small group where the use of dialect comes as a surprise, eg a lawyer in court defending a businessman accused of embezzling from his firm, or a headteacher addressing the parents of new pupils.

● Discuss whether you feel it causes problems when you speak in dialect in certain situations. Do you believe that people in particular jobs should be able to use a broad accent, or speak in dialect?

● How often do you come across dialect on television? Watch and listen carefully to one episode of an English soap and see how much dialect you can find. Remember you are looking for words and phrases that you don't use locally. Are there more examples than you ever realised or not as many as you expected? Which type of characters are shown to use most dialect? Watch and listen carefully to your local news magazine programme. How many local dialect words can you spot? Use the checklist on *Repromaster 34* to record your findings.

Local dialects are often treated as simply entertaining and looked down upon in a snobbish way. Many groups of people take the idea of the superiority of Standard English very seriously.

The poem which follows uses dialect not to entertain but to make a very serious point about the link which too many of us automatically make between the way people talk and the respect which their words deserve.

this is thi
six a clock
news thi
man said n
thi reason
a talk wia
BBC accent
iz coz yi
widny wahnt
mi ti talk
aboot thi
trooth wia
voice lik
wanna yoo
scruff. if
a toktaboot
thi trooth
lik wanna yoo
scruff yi
widny thingk
it wuz troo.
jist wanna yoo
scruff tokn.
thirza right
way ti spell
ana right way
ti tok it. this
is me tokn yir
right way a
spellin. this
is ma trooth.
yooz doant no
thi trooth
yirsellz cawz
yi canny talk
right. this is
the six a clock
nyooz. belt up.

Tom Leonard

● Conduct a community survey. What do people in your area feel about the use of dialect? Ask people from a wide range of ages and backgrounds. What local dialect can you collect? What about poetry and prose written in your local dialect? Is there a writer in the community who writes dialect poetry or a column in dialect in the local paper? Invite her/him into school. Write up a report about your findings and your opinions.

● Take a textbook of your choice, select a passage, and rewrite it in your local dialect. Be as accurate as you can. You might like to discuss your new version with the subject teacher.

Dub poetry is a new, exciting development in Nation Language. The name 'Dub poetry' comes from the way in which a reggae rhythm is 'dubbed' into the words of the poems. Dub poetry is very much intended to be performed in front of an audience, rather than read from a book, and all of the poets mentioned below have made recordings of their poetry with and without musical backing.

Linton Kwesi Johnson, born in Jamaica in 1952, but resident in England since 1963, published his first major collection of poetry in 1975. He is responsible for bringing much of the work of dub poets to the attention of the public. His written version of Nation Language is slightly different to that of the poets that follow.

Come Wi Goh Dung Deh

come wi goh dung deh
mek wi tek a ride dung deh
come wi goh dung deh
mek wi forwud dung deh
gonna badituppa badituppa badituppa . . .

come wi goh dung deh
de people demma bawl
fe foood dung deh
dem cant get noh food
but food dung deh

de people demma bawl
fe work dung deh
dem cant get noh work
but work dung deh

de people demma bawl
fe sheltah dung deh
dem cant get a room
but palace dung deh

de people demma bawl
fe mercy dung deh
dem cant get noh mercy
mercy noh dung deh . . .

come wi goh dung deh
mek wi tek a stride dung deh
come wi goh dung deh
mek wi forwud dung deh
gonna badituppa badituppa badituppa . . .

come wi goh dung deh

de people demma fite
fe work dung deh
de people dem a fite
one annadda dung deh

de people demma fite
fe stay alive dung deh
de people demma fite
fe dem rites dung deh

de people demma fite
oppreshan dung deh
de people demma fite
fe dem life dung deh

de people demma fite
fe suvvive dung deh
de people demma fite
demma fite dung deh

soh come wi goh dung deh
mek wi mek a stap dung deh
soh come wi goh dung deh
mek wi forwud dung deh
gonna badituppa badituppa badituppa . . .

come wi goh dung deh!

Linton Kwesi Johnson

Mutabaruka was born in Jamaica in 1952 and is very
exciting to watch in performance. Much of his poetry is
written in Standard English.

Nursery Rhyme Lament

first time
jack & jill
used to run up de hill everyday
now dem get pipe . . . an
water rate increase

everyday dem woulda
reincarnate humpty dumpty
fe fall off de wall

little bwoy blue
who loved to blow im horn
to de sheep in de meadow: little bwoy blue
grow up now . . . an
de sheep dem get curried
in a little cold suppa shop down de street

yu rememba when man was a ponder fe guh moon?
yet dem did 'ave de cat
fe play fiddle
so dat de cow coulda jump over it
every full moon . . . and
lite bill increase

den dere was
de ol' woman
who neva went to nuh fambly plannin clinic
she used to live someweh dung
back-o-wall inna one lef'-foot shoe
back-o-wall in fashion now . . . an
she move

jack sprat . . . ah, yes, jack sprat
who couldn't stand fat; im start eat it now . . . but
im son a vegetarian . . . 'cause
meat scarce

little bo-peep who lost 'ar sheep . . . went out
to look fe dem
an find instead a politician . . . and
is now livin in beverly hills

mary
(yu know 'ar . . . she had a white lamb)
well, she saw bo-peep
an decide she woulda give 'ar lamb
to cinderella godmother fe
change im colour to black
before midday . . . and
society grow

little jack
rememba im?
im use fe siddung a de corna
a king st. & barry st.
de adda day im put im thumb
inna im mout' . . . an
vomit . . . while
tom   tom   was   stealin a woman wig
im fall inna jack vomit . . . an
bruk im friggin neck

tom   tom   fada, de pied piper
turn pro now . . . an
stop blow to rats
but realize seh
nu rat neva falla im dung de rivva . . . an
im dead 'cause de clock strike 1:30 . . . an
nuh mous neva run down
                                    tic   toc   tic

first time
man use fe love dem
but dis is not de time fe dem . . . cause
dem deh days done
. . . . an wi write . . . .

Mutabaruka

Michael Smith was tragically killed in Jamaica in 1983 at the age of 28. He was stoned to death by a group of political fanatics after a political meeting at which he criticised the education system. Mi Cyaan Believe It is his best-known poem. It is probably the most important piece of dub poetry produced to date.

Mi Cyaan Believe It

Mi sey mi cyaan believe it
mi sey mi cyaan believe it

room dem a rent
mi apply widin
but as mi go in
cockroach rat an scarpian also come in

wan good nose hafi run
but mi na go
sidung pan 'igh wall like humty dumty
mi a face mi reality

one likkle bwoy come blow im 'orn
an mi look pan im wid scorn
an mi realize 'ow mi fine bwoy pickney
was a victim of de trix
dem call partisan pally-trix

an mi ban mi belly
an mi bawl
an mi ban mi belly
an mi bawl
lawd
mi cyaan believe it

mi sey mi cyaan believe it

Mi dawta bwoyfren name is sailor
an im pass through de port like a ship
more gran pickney fi feed
but de whole a wi need
wat a night wat a plight
an we cyaan get a bite/mi life is a stiff fite
an mi cyaan believe it

mi sey mi cyaan believe it

Sittin on de corner wid mi fren
talkin bout tings an time
mi a hear one voice say
'Who dat?'
mi sey 'a who dat?'
'A who a sey who dat
wen mi a sey who dat!'

When yu tek a stock
dem lick wi dung flat
teet start fly/an big man start cry
an mi cyaan believe it

mi sey mi cyaan believe it

De oder day mi pass one yard/pan de hill
when mi tek a stock
mi hear

Hi bwoy
yes mam
Hi bwoy
yes mam
Yu clean up de dwag shit?
yes mam
an mi cyaan believe it

mi sey mi cyaan believe it

Doris a moder a four
get a wuk as a domestic
boss man move in
an baps si sicai she pregnant again
baps si sicai she pregnant again
an mi cyaan believe it

mi sey mi cyaan believe it

Dah yard de oder nite when mi hear
fiah fiah to plate claat
Who dead?
You dead?
Who dead?
Mi dead?
Who dead?
Harry dead?
Who dead?
Eleven dead
Wooeeeeeeee
Orange Street fire dey pan mi head
an mi cyaan believe it

mi sey mi cyaan believe it

Lawd mi see some black bud livin ina one buildin
but nuh rent nuh pay/so dem cyaan stay
Lawd de oppress and de dispossess/cyaan get no rest
what next

tek a trip from Kingston
to Jamaica
tek twelve from a dozen
an mi see mi muma in heaven
. . . MAD OUSE

mi sey mi cyaan believe it
mi sey mi cyaan believe it

Yu believe it?
How yu fi believe it
when yu blind yu eye to it

But mi know yu believe it
Lawwwwwd
mi know yu believe it . . .

Michael Smith

*Benjamin Zephaniah is probably the best known dub poet
living and working in England today. He has done a lot of
work in schools and has appeared on several school
television programmes.*

Fight Dem, Not me

If you get uptight and you want to fight
fight dem, not me.
If you check out de scene and tings don't right
see dem, not me.
I came, I saw, I live here and I have my
tribulation to bear.
If you get uptight and you want to fight
fight dem, not me.

If you check history and you find a lie
see dem, not me.
And if you pay for the whole and but half is sold
check dem, not me.
I come from afar but I live here
and all I want is an equal share.
If you get uptight and you want to fight
fight dem, not me.
'Cause while you're fighting me,
dey will have time for corruption.
While you're fighting me,
dem will cook a' evil food.
Dey are the real racists.

Look at the way they oppose the immigration.
And to do their dirty work
dem make racists out of the youth.
So if you get uptight and you want to fight
fight dem,
you better fight dem,
no bother fight me,
not me,
not me.

Benjamin Zephaniah

Options

● The four dub poems might be described as 'statements of
protest'. Take each poem and list the things each poet is protesting
about or criticising.

● Which of these poems, in the opinion of your group, makes the
strongest statements of protest? List the poems in order of strength.

● List your comments/grievances about the state of the world, and
shape your ideas into a piece of prose or poetry in Nation Language,
in your own dialect, or in Standard English.

INTONATION

When we speak we use a changing pattern of sounds – sometimes long sounds and sometimes short. We place a greater accent or stress on certain sounds, and change the pitch in much the same way as music goes up and down. The word used to describe the 'music of speech' is intonation.

This can vary according to a person's accent, their mood or their attitude. Intonation also gives a clue to the type of sentence being spoken, whether (for example) a question is being asked, or a command is being given. Methods exist for translating the music of speech into symbols. • is used in the following examples to show which part of a word is given the most stress, while • is used to show which part is given the least. ⌐ or even ⌣ are used to indicate whether the voice rises or falls at that point. ═══ is the framework in which these marks are placed, and is used in a similar way to lines in music, to show the outer limits of the 'tune'.

Here are two examples:

over   *above*

When we really wish to add emphasis to our words, because we totally agree or disagree with something, the fall in our voice is sometimes greater, eg:

I do.

When we are being sarcastic or disbelieving, there may be a rise before the fall, eg:

No!   *Really!*

When our voices rise from mid to high pitch it shows eagerness, concern or questioning.

You did?

● With a partner, see if you can work out the symbols for the words 'good night', spoken in each of the following ways:
politely
cheerfully
unhappily
in a threatening manner
in a questioning manner.
Compare your results with the class.

That we can create a huge range of meanings for the same words, merely by changing the tone of our voices, can be seen easily from the following exercise.

Options

● With a partner see how many ways you can say the sentence: "She said this is what all the fuss was about."

Compare your results with the rest of the class.

● Take the following piece of dialogue, and act it out, with a partner.

You will have to have a clear picture in your mind of what is taking place.

1. How many
2. I don't know
1. Is it safe
2. So they say
1. This way

Act out your piece of script to another pair and compare stories. Share your results with the rest of the class.

● With a partner, produce a similar short piece of script. You must have some idea of a story clearly in mind but you should not give too many clues about the plot within your dialogue. Exchange scripts with another pair, and act out each other's scripts; then compare the two versions of each script, yours and theirs. What differences in intonation changed the story?

Just by listening carefully to intonation in speech, it is possible to decipher a huge complexity of attitudes, relationships, and moods, as well as gain a basic idea of what is being said, even in a language that is foreign to us.

Options

● Using only gibberish, improvise:
a) sharing a secret with a partner.
b) gossiping about a mutual friend.
c) boasting about something you have just bought.

In writing there is no way of showing intonation except perhaps by italics or capital letters, question marks or exclamation marks. Writing and speech are generally miles apart. In the following example, the writer is trying to reflect speech accurately, and to create other sounds in writing:

I'll soon be ome. You mustn't fret.
My feet's improvin', as I told you of.
We're out in rest now. Never fear.
(VRACH! By crumbs, but that was near.)

Wilfred Owen, *The Letter*

The way that onomatopoeic words (words that represent a sound, e g 'bang' or 'click') affect the tone of any sentence they appear in, is easy to see. But it is also possible to use certain letters or combinations of letters to create certain atmospheres: for example, the letters 's' and 'l' can convey a sleepy or peaceful atmosphere.

Many writers strive to capture natural speech; take a look at this 'conversation poem' by Michael Rosen. You might feel, however, that the extract from a play that follows, although exaggerated, is a more accurate picture of the way we use our voices.

Nothing Much

"What did you do on Friday?"
"Nothing much –
I like doing nothing quite often –

like putting on old hats
or drawing forests along the edges
of the newspapers we keep under the sink.
How about you?"

"I showed my mum and dad
what I had made in school that week.
It was a lorry
that works on elastic bands
and my dad said:
'What did you make that thing for?'
I bet he played with it when I went to bed."
Michael Rosen

The players examine their hands. When they talk, they do not look at each other, but concentrate entirely on their cards.

FIRST MAN (*humming softly as he sorts*): Pom-pom-pom-pom, pom-pom-pom, pom-pom-pom-pom, pom-pom-pom, pom-pom-pom-pom . . .
SECOND MAN (*whistling through his teeth*): Ss, ss-ss-ss-ss, ss-ss-ss, ss-ss-ss, ss-ss-ss, ss-ss-ss-ss . . .
FIRST LADY: Bub-bub-bub-bub, bub-bub-bub-bub, bub-bub-bub, bub-bub-bub-bub – whose call?
SECOND LADY: Your callikins.
FIRST LADY (*still engrossed in her cards*): My little callikins, well, well, well – *my* little callikins. Let me see, then, let me see – I think – I think – I think-a-pink-a-pink – no bid.
SECOND LADY: Tch-tch-tch, tch-tch-tch, tch-tch, tch-tch, tch-tch-tch, tch-tch-tch – no bid.
FIRST MAN: One cloob.
SECOND MAN (*dropping into Irish*): Did ye say one cloob?
FIRST MAN (*dropping into Irish*): I did that.
SECOND MAN: Er hat ein cloob gesagen. (*Singing*) Er hat ein cloob gesagen, er hat ein cloob . . . One hearty-party.
FIRST LADY: Two diminx.
SECOND LADY: No bid, no bid.

FIRST MAN: No bid-a-bid-bid.
SECOND MAN: Two diminx, is it? Two naughty leetle diminx. This, I think, demands a certain amount of consideration. (*Drums fingers on table*) Yes, yes, my friends, beaucoup de considération.
SECOND LADY (*after a pause*): Your *call*, partner.
SECOND MAN: I know it, I know it, I know it, I know it, I know it, indeed, indeed, I know it. (*Clacks tongue*) I know it, I know it, I double two diminx.
SECOND LADY: He doubles two diminx.
FIRST MAN: He doubles two diminx.
SECOND MAN: I double, I double, I double two diminx.
FIRST LADY: Very well, then, have at you. Two no trumpets.
FIRST MAN: Ha, ha!
SECOND MAN: Ho, ho!
FIRST LADY: He, he!
SECOND LADY: H'm, H'm!
They revert to their pet noises as they consider their hands.
Herbert Farjeon, *Nine Sharp*

Options

● Brainstorm as a class the differences between writing and speech.

● Tape-record and transcribe a small group in the class playing a card game or similar (allow them to relax into the activity before you begin recording), or record a similar situation at home (transcribe only with the family's permission).

● Write your own 'conversation poem' – aiming to produce something that is as close to natural speech as possible.

● Produce a piece of drama script in which the language used is as naturalistic as possible. Select a very ordinary daily occurrence to focus upon.

VARIATIONS

Dahn the Plug'ole

A muvver was barfin' 'er biby one night,
The youngest of ten and a tiny young mite,
The muvver was pore and the biby was thin,
Only a skelington covered in skin;
The muvver turned rahnd for the soap orf the rack,
She was but a moment, but when she turned back,
The biby was gorn; and in anguish she cried,
'Oh, where is my biby?' – the Angels replied:
'Your biby 'as fell dahn the plug'ole,
Your biby 'as gorn dahn the plug;
The poor little thing was so skinny and thin
'E oughter been barfed in a jug;
Your biby is perfectly 'appy,
'E won't need a barf any more,
Your baby 'as fell dahn the plug 'ole,
Not lorst, but gorn before!'
Anon

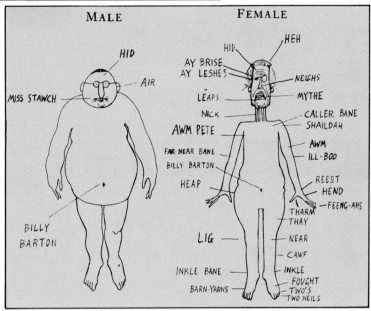

No Dialects Please

In this competition
dey was lookin for poetry of worth
for a writin that could wrap up a feelin
an fling it back hard
with a captive power to choke de stars
so dey say,
'Send them to us
but NO DIALECTS PLEASE'
We're British!

Ay!
Well ah laugh till me boushet near drop
Is not only dat ah tink
of de dialect of de Normans and de Saxons
dat combine an reformulate
to create a language-elect
is not only dat ah tink
how dis British education mus really be narrow
if it leave dem wid no knowledge
of what dey own history is about
is not only dat ah tink
bout de part of my story
dat come from Liverpool in a big dirty white ship
mark
AFRICAN SLAVES PLEASE!
We're the British!

But as if dat not enough pain
for a body to bear
ah tink bout de part on de plantations down dere
Wey dey so frighten o de power
in the deep spaces
behind our watching faces
dat dey shout

NO AFRICAN LANGUAGES PLEASE!
It's against the law!
Make me ha to go
an start up a language o me own
dat ah could share wid me people

Den when we start to shout
bout a culture o we own
a language o we own
a identity o we own
dem an de others dey leave to control us say
STOP THAT NONSENSE NOW
We're all British!
Every time we lif we foot to do we own ting
to fight we own fight
dey tell us how British we British
an ah wonder if dey remember
dat in Trinidad in the thirties
dey jail Butler
who dey sey is their British citizen
an accuse him of
Hampering the war effort!
Then it was
FIGHT FOR YOUR COUNTRY, FOLKS!
You're British!

Ay! Ay!
Ah wonder when it change to
NO DIALECTS PLEASE!
WE'RE British!
Huh!
To tink how still dey so dunce
an so frighten o we power
dat dey have to hide behind a language
that we could wrap roun we little finger
in addition to we own!
Heavens o mercy!
Dat is dunceness oui!
Ah wonder where is de bright British?

Merle Collins

Tottie

As she walked along the street
With her little plates of meat
And the summer sunshine falling on her golden
    Barnet Fair,
Bright as angels from the skies
Were her dark blue Mutton Pies;
In my East and West Dan Cupid shot a shaft and
    left it there.

She's a Grecian I suppose
And of Hampstead Heath two rows,
In her Sunny South they glistened like two pretty
    strings of pearls,
Down upon my bread and cheese
Did I drop and murmur, 'Please
Be my storm and strife, dear Tottie, O, you
    darlingest of girls.'

Then a bow wow by her side
Who 'til then had stood and tried
A Jenny Lee to banish, which was on his Jonah's
    Whale,
Gave a hydrophobia bark,
She cried, 'What a Noah's Ark,'
And right through my rank and riches did my
    cribbage pegs assail.

Ere her bull dog I could stop
She had called a ginger pop
Who said, 'What the Henry Meville do you think
    you're doing there?'
And I heard as off I slunk
'Why the fellow's Jumbo's trunk.'
And the Walter Joyce was Tottie's with the golden
    Barnet Fair . . .

Traditional English

A Gude Buke

Ah like a gude buke
a buke's aw ye need
jis settle doon
hiv a right gude read

Ay, a gude buke's rerr
it makes ye think
nuthin tae beat it
bar a gude drink

Ah like a gude buke
opens yir mine
a gude companion
tae pass the time

See me wi a buke, bit
in a bus ur a train
canny whack it
wee wurld i yir ain

Ay, ah like a gude buke
widny deny it
dje know thon wan
noo – whit dje cry it?

Awright pal, skip it
awright, keep the heid
howm ah tae know
yir tryin tae read

Stephen Mulrine

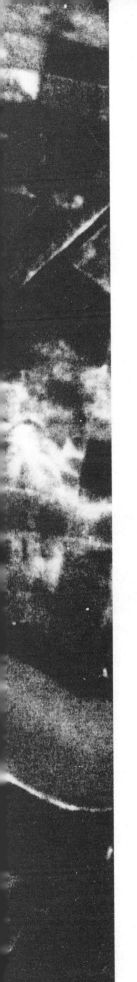

POWER & INFLUENCE

STEREOTYPE

When thinking about any particular type of person, whether they be old, rich, poor, famous, powerful, clever, northerners, southerners, foreigners or whatever, we use a kind of shorthand to help us create a picture in our minds. Each and every one of us has numerous words and phrases that are 'on the tips of our tongues', to describe hundreds of types of people. Try the following exercise to examine just how your ideas compare with the rest of the group.

● List, in pairs, the words and phrases which spring to mind when any of the following categories (or categories of your own) are mentioned:

1. Age	eg Kids …
2. Occupation	eg Office workers …
3. Accent	eg Geordies …
4. Place of origin	eg Londoners …
5. Social status	eg the Rich …
6. Character	eg Rough …
7. Education	eg Brainy …

Which of these does the class see as negative and which as positive?

It should be clear from your lists that we use our language in a very complicated way in order to 'place' people neatly in our minds. The pictures that we conjure up in our heads at the mere mention of one of these labels can be extremely detailed.

● In discussion groups, how much can you say about a typical:
a) football fan
b) rock star
c) 15-year-old
d) teacher.

Begin by making a list of, for example, types of clothes, hairstyles, behaviour, habits, common phrases they might use, and so on. You could even try a piece of roleplay using the four characters in order to build up a picture – they might be stuck in a lift together, for example.

When creating a picture of these four, what were you thinking of? People you know? Characters from television? Were you thinking about what you've read in magazines/ newspapers or about what people say in general about the characters? How closely do you fit in with the typical 15-year-old? Maybe some people in the class were slightly offended by your description.

In what way does a description of something that is 'typical' vary from a 'stereotype'? Which of the following definitions belongs to which: 'a fixed mental impression', 'representative'?

People are often judged simply on how they look. We often decide what a person is like before we even hear them speak. Just how accurate are those first impressions?

● Look at the photographs on this page. What stereotypes do you think they project? Select one word which describes the stereotype presented.

Using Repromaster 36 analyse the elements which go to make up the stereotype in each photograph.

How far are these stereotypes present in the media images that you see every day? Look at adverts, films and TV programmes, pop videos, LP sleeves, and magazines.

● You might like to use Repròmaster 36 to analyse other stereotypes. Choose a category (it might be based on age, geographical location, even hobbies) and collect stereotypical images and descriptions of people who fall into that category. Then work through the checklist on the repromaster to discover how these stereotypes are built up. When you have finished, you could write up a short report on your findings. Why, in your opinion, do people create and perpetuate these stereotypes?

Is stereotyping harmless or potentially dangerous? Are there certain types of stereotype that might be more dangerous than others? A very powerful stereotypical image of the way some men view women, in particular the way women talk, is represented in the rap poem following.

Men Talk

Women
Rabbit rabbit rabbit women
Tattle and titter
Women prattle
Women waffle and witter

Men Talk. Men Talk.

Women into Girl Talk
About Women's Trouble
Trivia 'n' Small Talk
They yap and they babble

Men Talk. Men Talk.

Women yatter
Women chatter
Women chew the fat, women spill the beans
Women aint been takin'
The oh-so Good Advice in them
Women's Magazines.

A Man Likes A Good Listener.

Oh yeah
I like A Woman
Who likes me enough
Not to nitpick
Not to nag and
Not to interrupt 'cause I call that treason
A woman with the Good Grace
To be struck dumb
By me Sweet Reason. Yes –

A Man Likes a Good Listener

A Real
Man
Likes a Real Good Listener
Women yap yap yap
Verbal Diarrhoea is a Female Disease
Woman she spread she rumours round she
Like Philadelphia Cream Cheese

Oh
Bossy Women Gossip
Girlish Women Giggle
Women natter, women nag
Women niggle niggle niggle

Men Talk.

Men
Think First, Speak Later
Men Talk.
Liz Lochhead

● Do you believe that the poet supports this attitude towards women? Why/why not?

● Using the rapping track on the tape, try and put together a rap about the rich/the poor, Southerners/Northerners, etc, in such a way that you make a mockery of stereotyping.

Popular television programmes often present stereotypes of people from other cultures or from various parts of the British Isles. Often such stereotypes cause offence amongst the groups which they are intended to represent. Explore this issue by trying the following activities.

Options

● Brainstorm examples of stereotypes from current soaps, situation comedies or television programmes, eg mothers-in-law, Asian shopkeepers, policemen. Then write a letter as a member of a particular social group that you feel has been negatively stereotyped on a current television soap, situation comedy or any other television programme.

● Write a discursive piece on the potential harm of stereotyping. Is the damage confined to those who are stereotyped?

HIDDEN MEANINGS

Many young people in Britain today are suffering daily because of racism. Sometimes racism can be very obvious, such as in name-calling or graffiti; at other times it can be slightly more subtle, as in the portrayal of Asian or Afro-Caribbean people as stupid or laughable in television or radio programmes. There are many examples, and all can be extremely hurtful. Many people suggest that even the English language itself can have a degrading effect on black people.

● Before you read on ... brainstorm with your class or group, phrases containing the word 'black' and phrases containing the word 'white'. Then decide which of the phrases are positive, which are neutral, and which are negative.

What, do you believe, might be the effects upon young people, black and white, growing up with a language that contains the examples that you have discovered?

Consulting a Thesaurus, Ossie Davies, an American black actor, discovered sixty negative phrases containing the word 'black' and ten negative phrases containing the word 'white'.

What do you make of the following extracts?

''Where I am is Africa,'' Ras Ibrahim and Ras Peter said, and they meant it. They carried the sense of their pre-exile days within them and without them, chieftains in Notting Hill Gate. They spoke a new language. Babylon's language was corrupt, full of imperial legacies that influenced thoughts. It took extreme sensitivity and awareness to speak without offending a black audience, and sensitivity and awareness were not qualities to be noted in white leaders.

Colette said that the English language was racist as well as sexist. Blackguard, blackmail, black spot, black sheep, black mark – even the Bible was full of people being washed whiter than snow, having their darkness lightened, asking the big white god to remove all dark passion from their souls.

R. Smith, *Rainbows of the Gutter*

The Change

Yesterday
God was
white.
Good was white,
so
white was right.

Yesterday
evil was
black
so
i took stock.
today,
I changed.

Mutabaruka

It might be argued that negative references to the word 'black' appeared long before Britain was a multicultural society. For example, 'black' itself actually comes from either of two Anglo Saxon words: *blāce* (meaning 'dark') and *blác* (meaning 'shining' or 'white' – the word 'bleach' comes from this source). So 'blackmail' is so called because it's paid in *shining* coins. In addition, the association of evil and darkness is said to spring from a fear of the night.

● How do you react to this information? Does it affect your opinions in any way?

● Examine a selection of books intended for young children in your local library. How are non-white characters presented? Look for good examples of a positive portrait of a multicultural society.

- Explore comics for non-white characters. Examine the language they use and the roles they play. What are your conclusions about the way comics represent a multicultural society? Are non-whites presented equally and positively? How might the way non-whites are shown affect the attitudes of readers? You might be interested to know that young people spend three times as much money on comics as they do on books. Examine adult comics and newspaper comic strips too. Discuss, and then write about your thoughts on the matter.

- As a result of your research into newspaper comic strips, write a letter to a particular editor, or to the Press Council (the 'watchdog' of newspapers) expressing your opinions.

In literature, disturbing messages, linking the colour of a person's skin to superiority or inferiority, can be passed on to young people. The following is one example.

The story is about a Robinson Crusoe-type figure called Miss Pettifer and her cat MacKenzie. This extract tells what happened when the inhabitants of a nearby island arrived and discovered Miss Pettifer's garden:

(they) began to shriek and jabber, pointing at it and pulling the flowers – stamping on the flower beds with their wide flat feet. Miss Pettifer ground her teeth with indignation.

When they caught sight of the fire, the effect was electric. Every savage sprang back and seized his spear or his knobkerry. A deathly silence fell upon them as their heads moved this way and that as if on stalks – seeking danger.

Then, as nothing happened, down on their hands and knees went the whole party, snuffling and pointing at the footprints and paw-marks of Miss Pettifer and MacKenzie which covered the sands . . .

Ursula Moray Williams, *The Nine Lives of Island MacKenzie*

- Which of the words that are used here give a negative idea of the visitors? What, do you think, are the possible effects of such books?

To be bilingual or multilingual is to be extremely gifted. To be able to communicate in two or more languages is something many people would love to be able to do.

On the tape you can hear young people talking about the other languages they speak – Welsh and Gaelic. Many of them feel that although these languages are under threat they are still part of their cultural heritage and their identity.

But researchers have discovered that many British Asian children keep their two (or more) languages completely separate. In school, they use only English; no one shows any appreciation or understanding of their 'mother tongue'. As a result they believe that British society considers the language of their parents to be inferior. In this way, they learn to devalue their own racial identity.

Similarly, children of West Indian parents often have their own variety of language criticised. What do you feel about the following?

The kind of English he spoke was not quite the kind of English most of the children spoke.

At news time in class Luke said something like, "Yesterday I go to de park, and I play wid de baby." Only a few children laughed, but a few were too many. The teacher did not laugh at all, but only corrected him: "Yesterday I went to the park, and I played with the baby. Say 'th', Luke, with your tongue between your teeth."

Luke swallowed hard. He did not see the point of what she was saying.

"Come along, Luke, lots of people from other countries can't say 'th' when they first come."

But Luke did not think he was learning the language, he thought he knew it, and he was angry and worried.

"Just try," said the teacher, and everybody waited. "Tongue between your teeth."

Luke scowled and thought it was a fuss about nothing, but he said, "Th."

"Again."

Luke clenched his fists under the desk. "Th."

"That's right. Now, when you get home, practise it and use it in words. Let's all try a few 'th' words. I'll write them on the board. Say them after me."

Mary Cockett, *Another Home, Another Country*

- If possible, interview a bilingual child about their experiences in and out of school. Write up the interview, adding your personal responses.

HIDDEN MEANINGS 2

"Until quite recently the language used to describe positions of power has been very much male-orientated – for example, 'head*master*' and 'chair*man*'. As both of these positions are often occupied by women, 'headteacher' and 'chair' or 'chairperson' are now very often used. Unfortunately, that is not the end of the problem. The English language still contains many sexist influences."

Options

● What do you think of this statement?

© Posy Simmonds 1987

● In a brainstorming exercise, collect together words or phrases with the word 'man' in, then do the same for the word 'woman'. Decide which are negative, which are neutral and which are positive. Here are a few to start with: 'man of the world', 'manpower', 'craftsman', 'landlady', 'woman of the streets', 'charlady'.

● In another brainstorming exercise consider the language used when women and men are described negatively. Which set of words is most powerful and hurtful?

● Try 'turning the world upside down' yourself. Roleplay a group of women at a bar in a disco discussing men as they enter, or a group of women discussing men drivers. Can you think of other situations in which we might hear sexist stereotyping? You might even like to prepare a drama script based on your ideas.

● In discussion groups: how many 'useless' women and girls can you find in nursery rhymes? How do men and boys figure? This is a very simple form of literature; do you feel that it can have any effect on people's attitudes?

● What about the following piece of literature? What are your feelings about the language used and the ideas expressed?

George cut the cards and began turning them over, looking at each one and throwing it down on a pile. He said: "This guy Curley sounds like a son-of-a-bitch to me. I don't like mean little guys."

"Seems to me like he's worse lately," said the swamper. "He got married a couple of weeks ago. Wife lives over in the boss's house. Seems like Curley is cockier'n ever since he got married."

George grunted: "Maybe he's showin' off for his wife."

The swamper warmed to his gossip. "You seen that glove on his left hand."

"Yeah. I seen it."

"Well, I tell ya what, Curley says he's keepin' that hand soft for his wife."

George studied the cards absorbedly. 'That's a dirty thing to tell around," he said.

The old man was reassured. He had drawn a derogatory statement from George. He felt safe now, and he spoke more confidently. "Wait'll you see Curley's wife."

George cut the cards again and put out a solitaire lay, slowly and deliberately. "Purty?" he asked casually.

"Yeah. Purty . . . but . . ."

George studied his cards. "But what?"

"Well – she got the eye."

"Yeah? Married two weeks and got the eye? Maybe that's why Curley's pants is full of ants."

"I seen her give Slim the eye. Slim's a jerkline skinner. Hell of a nice fella. Slim don't need to wear no high-heeled boots on a grain team. I seen her give Slim the eye. Curley never seen it. An' I seen her give Carlson the eye."

George pretended a lack of interest. "Looks like we was gonna have fun."

The swamper stood up from his box. "Know what I think?" George did not answer. "Well, I think Curley's married . . . a tart."

"He ain't the first," said George. "There's plenty done that."

John Steinbeck, *Of Mice and Men*

● In discussion groups examine the language of the advertisement below.
To whom is the message directed?
Do you find the ideas behind the advertisement and the language used clever/effective/offensive/humorous/subtle?

● You might like to produce a similar storyline to sell a product, or produce a send-up of this style of advertising.

Just looking at her makes me feel young again

It happened one Friday. Lunch had been sacrificed to yet another in a string of dreary meetings. My brain was whimpering "Enough!", when I became aware of her keys in my pocket, offering escape. It was just what I needed.

With her, the drive home seemed very quick, even in Friday traffic. "Unsettled everywhere" chimed the weatherman cheerily over the radio-cassette's six speakers, so umbrellas and extra books went in the back while our overnight bags disappeared into the vastness of the boot. Then, tempting fate, I opened the sunroof and we headed west. I used to take impromptu trips often once, back when my responsibilities were few. I had a little roadster then, my pride and joy, even though the thrill of the wind in my hair was somewhat undone by the draught up my trouser leg. A far cry from the splendid hush of my new Rover 820 Si. True, it's unfair to compare the two; infra-red remote central locking was the stuff of science fiction then. Also, my expectations in life are greater now, which is why I take such pleasure in the thoughtful Rover luxuries my £14,699 bought. Like heated electric door mirrors, electric mirrors all round, steering wheel and driver's seat each height adjustable.

And yet, winding over those familiar hills out of Bala, I couldn't help reminiscing on the fun of driving that roadster. I realised that of all the cars I'd had since, only this Rover made me feel as good behind the wheel. And thanks to Rover's sophisticated new electronic fuel injection system, she never wants for power, even when cold. Which is more than I can say for the last few cars I've driven. It seems that in the past, I've always gone for the temperamental type, and not only in cars. But as we rounded the point to the hotel that evening, I knew I'd finally got things right.

● You might like to draw your ideas together on 'Hidden Meanings' from the activities on the last four pages, and write a discursive piece covering 'Language: race and gender'.

READ ALL ABOUT IT

Headlines are designed to attract attention and to sell newspapers. The headlines in some newspapers are larger and far more dramatic than in others, and very often give completely different impressions of the same item of news. (The contents of the stories may be very different too, of course.) The differences may be due to the particular political bias of the newspaper, or due to the sensationalist nature of the newspaper. It would seem to be a fact of life that headlines which scream about violence, sex, crime and death fill many of our most popular newspapers. The motivation behind these headlines is probably the desire to create an emotional response.

Options

● Discuss with a partner why such headlines are the most common.

● Look at the contrasting headlines below. Discuss what different messages they are sending.

ENGLAND FANS IN RIOT SHAME

Terror ambush after big match

Fans ambushed by German mob

Battle in Stuttgart

Nazis ambush British gangs

Ban the yobs from travel

TERROR ATTACK BY FANTASY GUNMAN

Prison riot mob besiege troops

LOCK UP YOUR KIDS

KILLER

TERROR

BATTERED TO DEATH

● With a partner examine one issue of a popular tabloid newspaper and one issue of a serious newspaper, and compare the differing headlines for the same stories. Try and work out the reasons why they are different.

● Using a number of headlines from either type of newspaper, produce a cut-up poem, like the example below, that captures the style of the newspaper.

TERROR **PAIN!**

Vicious raid

VIOLENT THUGS RIOT SHAME

Missing son

police rescue bid

GUNMAN on streets

LOCK UP YOUR KIDS

SUICIDE SHAMEFUL

DYING MAN ADMITS

- Select a particular theme of headline from a collection of tabloids and produce a collage. Call it 'The Language of ——— .' Write about how you feel about the way 'The Language of ———' fills our newspapers. Imagine that this will be the editorial of a brand new newspaper designed to report only good news – 'The Good Times'? Think up some dramatic but positive headlines. (You could even extend them into stories.)

As well as the wording of a news story, and its headline, the amount of space given to a particular news story in a particular newspaper, its position in the newspaper, and the selection of facts given, says a great deal about the newspaper's policies and politics.

Options

- Compare your tabloid and serious newspaper again and discuss the points raised above.

- Select a topic that is currently in the news and produce three short news items: one to show strong approval, one to show strong disapproval and one that is neutral.

Many headlines are often impossible to decipher without knowing the full story. The overall effect of a headline without a story can be quite bizarre.

- Using the headlines shown here, or any that you can find yourself, create a bizarre news story.

'Hostile', 'inaccurate', 'greedy' and 'full of errors' are some of the comments made about newspapers by people throughout history. What are your opinions? Can you think of any personalities who have recently received hostile treatment in the press? Have your previous discussions led you to believe that greed is the main reason for dramatic headlines? Are you aware that each year the Press Council investigates hundreds of complaints about inaccuracies, and that sometimes stories are found to be completely false?

''Have you noticed that life, real honest-to-goodness life, with murders and catastrophes and fabulous inheritances, happens almost exclusively in the newspapers?''
Jean Anouilh

''The evil that men do lives on the front pages of greedy newspapers, but the good is oft interred apathetically inside.''
Brooks Atkinson, 1950

''Four hostile newspapers are more to be feared than a thousand bayonets.''
Napoleon I, 1815

''The man who never looks into a newspaper is better informed than he who reads them; inasmuch as he who knows nothing is nearer to the truth than he whose mind is filled with falsehood and errors.''
Thomas Jefferson, 1805

Options

- In your groups discuss these quotations. Which do you think comes nearest to the truth?

- Reduce the quotation of your choice to a short headline and write an article on the theme.

THE NAME GAME

What's in a name?

"That which we call a rose, By any other name would smell as sweet."
William Shakespeare

"The beginning of a wise policy is to call things by their right name."
17th-century Chinese

What do you make of these two statements? How important are the names we give to things? The fact that we have different names for the same thing can sometimes be simply confusing or annoying. Valerie Bloom writes about one example.

Wha Fe Call I'

Miss Ivy, tell me supmn,
An mi wan', yuh ansa good.
When yuh eat roun 12 o'clock,
Wassit yuh call yuh food?

For fram mi come yah mi confuse,
An mi noh know which is right,
Weddah dinnah a de food yuh eat midday,
Or de one yuh eat a night.

Mi know sey breakfus a de mawnin one
But cyan tell ef suppa a six or t'ree,
An one ting mi wi nebba undastan,
Is when yuh hab yuh tea.

Miss A dung a London ha lunch 12 o'clock,
An dinnah she hab bout t'ree,
Suppa she hab bout six o'clock,
But she noh hab noh tea.

Den mi go a Cambridge todda day,
Wi hab dinnah roun' bout two,
T'ree hour later mi frien she sey,
Mi hungry, how bout yuh?

Joe sey im tink a suppa time,
An mi sey yes, mi agree,
She halla, "Suppa? a five o'clock,
Missis yuh mussa mean tea!"

Den Sunday mi employer get up late,
Soh she noh hab breakfus nor lunch,
But mi hear she a talk bout 'Elevenses',
At one sinting dem call 'Brunch'.

Breakfus, elevenses, an brunch,
Lunch, dinnah, suppa, tea,
Mi brain cyan wuk out which is which,
An when a de time fe hab i'.

For jus' when mi mek headway,
Sinting dreadful set mi back,
An dis when mi tink mi know dem all,
Mi hear bout one name snack.

Mi noh tink mi a badda wid no name,
Mi dis a nyam when time mi hungry,
For doah mi 'tomach wi glad fe de food,
I' couldn care less whey mi call i'.
Valerie Bloom

Sometimes, however, we deliberately avoid the real name of something and give it a different name – sometimes several different names. These are called euphemisms. We use them sometimes to be polite, sometimes to avoid referring directly to something which is regarded as unpleasant or dirty, frightening, rude or sensitive. For example, death is often referred to as 'passing away', 'going to the other side' or 'meeting one's maker'. Undertakers have become 'funeral directors', dustbinmen 'refuse collectors', sweat is referred to as 'perspiration' or 'body odour'. Toilet probably wins the prize as the most avoided word with euphemisms such as 'privy', 'W.C.', 'loo', 'powder room', 'bogs', 'ladies', 'gents', 'conveniences'. What other examples of euphemisms can you think of?

● Roleplay a conversation between two people, both of whom are dealing with one of the sensitive words mentioned above or one you came up with in your discussions. During the conversation the sensitive word must not be mentioned. See how inventive you can be.

Sometimes the Powers That Be decide that there are particular words or phrases that we shouldn't concern ourselves with for fear that we might not be able to cope with the reality behind them. The naked truth is hidden from view behind a mask. During the war in Vietnam, the verb 'to kill' was often replaced by 'to neutralise', or even 'to off'. In other recent wars, we have heard of the 'pre-emptive strike', meaning a surprise attack, 'air support', meaning bombing, and 'accelerated pacification', meaning intensive bombing. An 'anti-personnel weapon' is one that destroys people – soldiers or civilians.

Another typically military use of language is the use of 'acronyms', words formed from the initial letters of other words. The modern military uses dozens of them.

● Discuss the military use of 'euphemisms' and 'acronyms'. Do you believe that this represents an attempt to 'play down' weapons, war and the threat of war?

Language can be used to distort the truth, either by softening the message, as we have seen with euphemisms, or by exaggeration. The same story in two different newspapers may be very different, depending upon what they think their readers want to read.

Options

● Compare an up-to-the-minute news story in the same day's tabloids and serious newspapers. Discuss the differences in the use of language and presentation.

● Choose a headline from a serious newspaper and write a short, factual article based on it; then write the same story with an exciting headline and using highly dramatic language.

● Write about an occasion when you have over-exaggerated or played down an event to your family or friends. End your personal account with a description of your feelings or thoughts – at the time of the incident, and at present.

Distorting the facts behind a story is an everyday occurrence – take rumours and gossip, for example. The following exercise is intended to encourage you to explore an occasion when you yourself may have been guilty of distortion.

● Roleplay a situation where a fifth former is giving an account to a reporter about a riot in school; his/her account will be very vivid. Now change roles, and as a headteacher, 'play down' the riot to the same reporter.

Language can be used to carry a powerful political message: for example, in a particular country terrorists may be known as freedom fighters, aggression and violence known as liberation.

GETTING YOUR POINT ACROSS

When we talk, we use many gestures in order to get our points across. In a famous study of human habits, **Manwatching**, *Desmond Morris analyses the gestures that we make.*

Options

● Before you read the explanations on *Repromaster 37*, try to work out the meanings of the gestures.

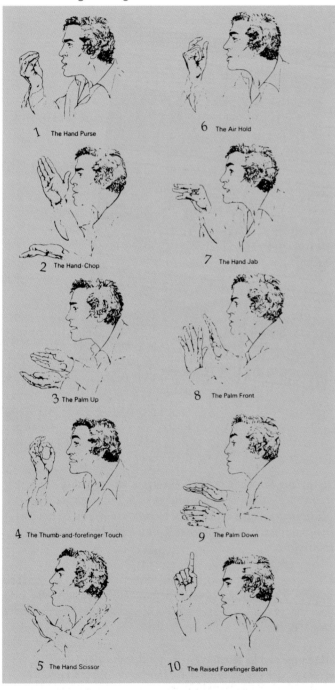

1 The Hand Purse

6 The Air Hold

2 The Hand-Chop

7 The Hand Jab

3 The Palm Up

8 The Palm Front

4 The Thumb-and-forefinger Touch

9 The Palm Down

5 The Hand Scissor

10 The Raised Forefinger Baton

● Using the notes 1–10 on the repromaster, work out, with a partner, a sentence that might be spoken with each gesture.

How well did you interpret the gestures? Do your sentences fit in with the explanations?

Desmond Morris points out that these gestures have become so important to us as a way of getting points across that we even use them when we're on the telephone! In the following extract from **Manwatching** *he makes several other interesting points.*

The term he uses to describe hand gestures is 'batoning'. He also uses a more general term, 'gesticulating'. With the help of this brief explanation, can you make sense of the following passage?

Apart from group-to-group differences and person-to-person differences, there are also variations in batoning frequency from occasion to occasion for the same individual. Since batons are concerned with both emphasis and mood, it follows that in situations where spoken comments are rather matter-of-fact, such as when ordering groceries, the words will be accompanied by fewer batons than when someone is arguing about some passionately held belief. Also, he is more likely to gesticulate if he is an enthusiast rather than a cynic. The enthusiast wants to share his excitements and feels a powerful need to emphasise every point that he considers important. The cynic is so negative in all his attitudes that he feels no such urge.

The enthusiast's behaviour provides another clue. His batons beat out his eagerness to arouse similar enthusiasm in his listeners. The more feedback he gets from them, the more successful he will feel. The more successful he feels, the less he will be driven – unconsciously – to emphasise his verbal statements. So, the reaction of his audience to his speech is a vital factor in influencing the intensity of his baton signals. A demonstrative and totally sympathetic listener will tend to damp down his gesticulations. But give him an attentive yet critical audience and his hands will start to dance. He must win over the listener and to do this he must emphasise his words over and over again. Bearing this in mind, it suddenly becomes clear why public speakers addressing large groups of people gesticulate so much more than private conversationalists. The same man talking to a single friend or addressing a big audience shows many more batons in the public situation than in the private encounter. The reason is that, paradoxically, he gets less feedback from the crowd than he does from the solitary friend. The friend keeps on nodding and smiling and the speaker knows all the time that his words are getting across. No need then to add much manual emphasis. But the members of a large audience do not show their minute-by-minute appreciation with smiles and nods. Being part of a crowd makes their relationship with the speaker impersonal. They stare at him and save their reaction for the end, when they applaud with hand-clapping. For the speaker, the sea of faces is a challenge – they are not nodding as a close friend would do, so what precisely *are* they thinking? Are the ideas getting across or are they failing to make any impact? Unconsciously, the speaker decides that the only safe course of action is to step up the emphasis, just to make sure. And so it is that moderate gesticulators in private become intense gesticulators on the public platform.

Finally, in addition to differences in frequency, there is also much subtle variation in baton style. But little research has been done on this subject so far, and for a detailed report on baton 'dialects', we must await the results of field studies yet to come.

Desmond Morris, *Manwatching*

● With a partner list all the examples the writer gives of situations where gestures are used more than normal. Then list all the examples of situations when gestures are used less than normal. Can you think of any other occasions?

Physical gestures are only one way of attempting to get our points across. Politicians are professionals, and, one might say, will almost stop at nothing to persuade people to vote for them. The following is an account of the election campaign of an American politician, Mr A. B. (Happy) Chandler, in 1963.

He evokes cheers and tears from his audience with equal ease, and does not hesitate to shout and weep with them. He quotes (or misquotes) the Bible, Shakespeare or his Uncle Ben with equal facility, calls on the Lord frequently and with easy familiarity . . . If the day is warm, he throws aside his jacket and loosens his tie before addressing the faithful . . . On the platform beneath the trees of the courthouse lawn, he manages to hug each local dignitary, all the while calling and waving to the audience, ''Hello, there, John,'' ''Howdy, Bob,'' ''Hello, there, Preacher.''

There may not be a John, Bob, Tom or Preacher in the audience, but if there is, he will be sure that Happy's greeting is for him alone. Happy knows this . . . After a prayer and eulogies by local supporters, he gets down to business. If he feels he has his opponents on the run, he launches into a burst of scorn and ridicule; but if he is himself under fire he likes to divert his listeners by an appeal to emotion. Once . . . he interrupted his explanation because, he said, he had just spotted a 'dear little, grey-haired lady' in the audience, whose face had taken him back to the days of the war. He described how he went to North Africa 'to see how they were treating our boys'. There he made his way to the front line.

''And suddenly,'' he recounted, '' I saw this fine young boy, lying wounded there on the ground, and he looked up at me and said: 'Why, it's Happy Chandler!'

'' 'Yes, son,' I said, and he reached out his hand and he said, 'I'm from Kentucky, Happy.' And I knelt down there on the sand beside him, and I could see the hand was on him, and he was about to cross over, and he reached out and said, 'Take my hand, Happy, 'cause I'm about to go.'

''I'm not ashamed to say there were tears on my face as I held the hand of that brave boy, dying there so far from the old Kentucky home he loved, and he said to me, he said, 'Happy, I want you to promise me you'll take word back for me, 'cause there's a sweet little old lady waiting for me, and I'm not coming home. Tell her I died facing the enemy, Happy, but thinking of home.' And I said, 'I'll do it, son.' ''

The story continued with his return to Kentucky and a visit to the 'sweet little Kentucky mother'. Then he stepped down and led to the platform a small greying woman, weeping copiously, and with his arm round her shoulders he faced the audience. By this time there was hardly a dry eye in the crowd.

The Times, 5 March 1963

Options

● Build up to writing a similar political speech about yourself by first trying the following exercises.

● Work with a partner. One must clench a fist in anger, the other has to persuade that person to unclench it.

● Both of you and your partner must choose a colour (your favourite colours, if they are not the same) and persuade each other that your own personal choice is vastly superior.

● Convince your partner that they should buy the chair you're sitting on.

You might find it interesting to have a third person with each pair simply observing the gestures (write down the number of gestures used) and any verbal tricks and ploys that you resort to. Use the gestures checklist on *Repromaster 38* to record your findings.

● Play the famous 'fall-out shelter' game. Eight or ten of you are in a fall-out shelter, with only limited supplies of food. Three or four must leave the shelter in order that the remainder might survive. Each group member must take on the identity of a famous person, or a person with a particular profession. In turn, each must persuade the others that they deserve to live. Ultimately a vote is taken.

● Now make your own political speech urging people to vote for you in the forthcoming general/local council/school council elections. Use any ploy you can think of in order to gain votes.

THE POWER OF PERSUASION

Pamphlets protesting about a wide variety of things ranging from abortion to smoking, from bloodsports to the dumping of nuclear waste, are common in modern day society. They are designed to have a powerful impact, and aim to open peoples' eyes or change attitudes. They have become an art form in themselves. Below are just a few examples for you to study. You may be able to collect more yourselves.

"I cannot think of a single major breakthrough that was produced as a result of an animal experiment. I wonder how many more million animals have to be sacrificed before we abandon the useless and barbaric practice of animal experimentation."

Dr. Vernon Coleman,
Fellow of the Royal Society of Medicine

Every year in Britain alone millions of animals suffer and die in laboratory experiments. They are burned, blinded, scalded, poisoned and infected with diseases. They are shocked, irradiated and gassed. In most cases no pain relief is given. Behind the closed, locked doors of British laboratories they suffer in silence: death is the only release.

History shows that the experiments are doubly absurd. For vivisection is not only irrelevant to real advances in health but results are often dangerously misleading. Opren, Eraldin and Flosint are all cases of animal-tested drugs which had to be withdrawn because they caused suffering and death in humans.

Important advances continue to be made using methods which are both humane and directly applicable to people. And doctors have learnt how to prevent serious illnesses like cancer and heart disease by observation of human beings rather than through experiments on animals. Yet every hour of every day another 20,000 animals die in the world's laboratories.

**Animal experiments –
There is no need for them.
There is no place for them.
There is a choice!**

Ring or write now for your free information pack.

British Union for the Abolition of Vivisection
16a Crane Grove,
London N7 8LB
01-700 4888

BUAV AGAINST ALL ANIMAL EXPERIMENTS

13

I'd like to know more.
Please send me my free Information Pack

Name _____

Address _____

_____

Please accept my donation of £ _____
towards your work.

Please make cheques/P.O. payable to BUAV

13

☐ I would like to join the BUAV
I endorse the object of the British Union for the Abolition of Vivisection.

☐ I enclose cheque/P.O. for £ _____
£6.00 Annual Subscription (£3.00 unwaged)
£100.00 Life Membership.

Name (Mr/Ms) _____

Address _____

Signed _____ Date _____

COSMETICS
ALL
WEAPONS
THESE
MEDICINES
PRODUCTS
PAINTS
ARE
SHAMPOO
TESTED ON
WEEDKILLER
ANIMALS

Options

● With a partner, look carefully at the examples of protest and campaigning pamphlets above, and on *Repromaster 39* List the particular features of the pamphlets that you feel help to put the message across well. Arrange the list in order of importance. Does one pamphlet succeed more than the others in getting its message across? Why? Are any of the examples over-dramatic? Will any of them defeat their purpose and simply antagonise people? What is your attitude, your family's attitude, your friends' attitudes towards having protest leaflets given or delivered to your door?

● Create your own protest leaflet, paying attention to the need for the kind of strong, dramatic language used in the examples as well as eyecatching headlines, graphics and powerful visual images. You will need to research your subject well and plan the layout and content carefully. You may choose foxhunting, vivisection, nuclear energy, smoking, pollution, the dumping of waste, the building of a new motorway through a local village, the slaughter of whales, the culling of seals, battery farming, or any other issue about which you have strong feelings.

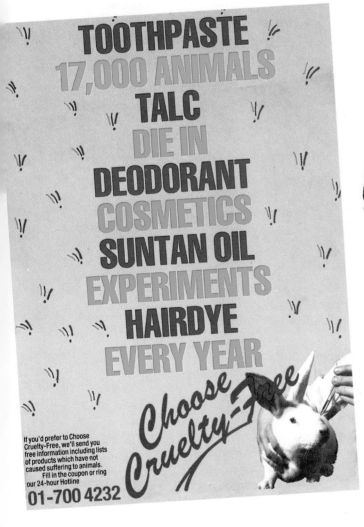

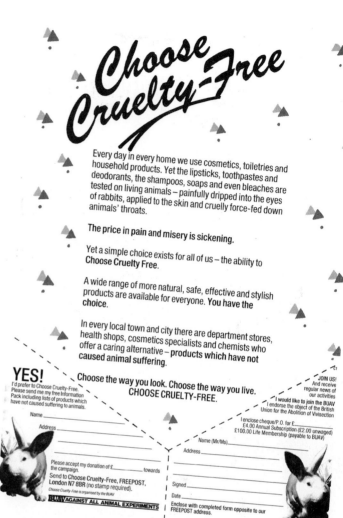

● Roleplay a meeting at which, for example, a group of foxhunters put forward the arguments in favour of foxhunting and a group in the audience, who are opposed to foxhunting, make their feelings known. You could try the same thing with vivisection, nuclear energy, smoking, or local issues. The research you have done in preparation for your leaflet will be vitally important.

● When you have completed these activities, write an extended discursive piece, giving the case for and against your chosen subject, ending up with your personal opinions stated firmly and clearly as the conclusion. For the purposes of this exercise be careful not to go over the top. Be cool, calm, but persuasive.

● Use your protest leaflet as the basis of an individual talk you might give in front of the class. Alternatively, use it as the starting point of a formal class debate.

THE POWER OF ADVERTISING

Advertisers use various devices to draw our attention to a product and entice us to use it. Of course, language plays a major part in this.

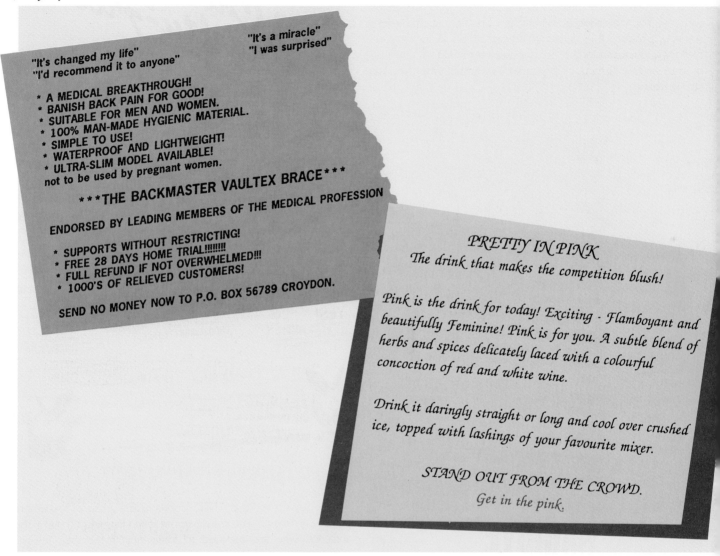

"It's changed my life"
"I'd recommend it to anyone"

"It's a miracle"
"I was surprised"

* A MEDICAL BREAKTHROUGH!
* BANISH BACK PAIN FOR GOOD!
* SUITABLE FOR MEN AND WOMEN.
* 100% MAN-MADE HYGIENIC MATERIAL.
* SIMPLE TO USE!
* WATERPROOF AND LIGHTWEIGHT!
* ULTRA-SLIM MODEL AVAILABLE!
not to be used by pregnant women.

THE BACKMASTER VAULTEX BRACE

ENDORSED BY LEADING MEMBERS OF THE MEDICAL PROFESSION

* SUPPORTS WITHOUT RESTRICTING!
* FREE 28 DAYS HOME TRIAL!!!!!!!!
* FULL REFUND IF NOT OVERWHELMED!!!
* 1000'S OF RELIEVED CUSTOMERS!

SEND NO MONEY NOW TO P.O. BOX 56789 CROYDON.

PRETTY IN PINK
The drink that makes the competition blush!

Pink is the drink for today! Exciting - Flamboyant and beautifully Feminine! Pink is for you. A subtle blend of herbs and spices delicately laced with a colourful concoction of red and white wine.

Drink it daringly straight or long and cool over crushed ice, topped with lashings of your favourite mixer.

STAND OUT FROM THE CROWD.
Get in the pink.

Often the language is emotive, over-the-top, or full of clichés (phrases so over-used that they have little meaning left).

Language is used to tempt, to persuade, even to blackmail us into believing that we should be ashamed of ourselves for not buying a certain product for ourselves or for our families. Advertisers expect us to believe 'what the experts say' about their products. They challenge us to 'keep up to date', 'keep up with the neighbours', or even 'keep one jump ahead'. They promise that our lives will dramatically improve and our attractiveness to other people will increase. They offer us 'great value', 'mammoth savings' and 'bargains of the century'. They make us feel stupid or inferior for even dreaming of using someone else's product. As far as health, insurance or educational products are concerned, we are made to feel morally in the wrong if we fail to leap at the opportunity being offered to us.

Options

● Examine the examples of advertisers' language above. What is each advertisement suggesting to the consumer?

● With a partner, look for examples of language that fall into the categories mentioned in the introduction. What devices are the advertisers using to encourage the customer to spend money? Make a list of these devices and note down any comments you wish to make about the advertisements. Report back to the class.

You will never have seen the adverts shown here in magazines or newspapers. They have been devised simply to show you how the language of advertising works, and the products advertised are not genuine. But if you think that the language used is a little over-the-top, try comparing the examples on this page with the wording of genuine adverts.

STALLION V.I.P.
(MORE EXTRAS THAN BEN HURR)

The Stallion is the ultimate chariot. A unique combination of design and technology, it re-captures the thrill of driving without compromising comfort and style. A V8 3000cc engine delivers a staggering 402 brake horse power of pure thrust (that's 400 more horse power than Ben Hurr ever had). Included as standard are: power steering, ABS Brakes, sunroof, stereo, car phone, alloy wheels. . . the list goes on.

The new H reg model is waiting. Take the reins if you dare.

FREE CONNECTION

FREE DELIVERY

EXPERT ADVICE

pay nothing

FREE HOTLINE

fits the British way of life.

SHE'S . GOT . IT

HAVE . YOU . GOT . IT?

NOT A PENNY MORE TO PAY

BIG SAVINGS

FREE OFFERS

PHONE A LOAN

YOURS TODAY

● In a group, make a collage of magazine advertisements with a common theme, eg directed at making the consumer more attractive, more healthy, improving his/her social status, etc.

'Cheap Woollen Hats for Bald Old Men' is a highly unlikely combination of words for an advertisement. For obvious reasons many words are avoided.

● Imagine that no one had to go to school. Produce an advertisement promoting education and the benefits of attending school. Who would you direct it towards? Parents? Children themselves? What devices would you use? What styles of language?

● Using what you have discovered, write a discursive piece with the title 'The Language of Advertising'. Give a general description of the variety of types of advertising language you have found; you could also include advice for consumers to help them avoid being taken in. In addition, you could incorporate your cut-up poem, list of clichés, and so on.

● Write a letter to the Advertising Standards Authority complaining about the devices used to persuade people to buy certain products. You could draw your examples from the collage you may have produced earlier. Interview family, friends and members of the local community so that you can quote the opinions of others.

THE WRITING ON THE WALL

Since prehistoric times, humanity has had the burning desire to communicate by scrawling on walls. The earliest examples range from simple handprints, outlined with chalk and charcoal, to pictures of the animals hunted by early peoples. These pictures are thought to represent a sort of hunting magic: prehistoric hunters believed that if they drew pictures of their prey, then they would gain more control over the real thing. By Egyptian times, the beautiful drawings had developed into 'pictographs' (pictures that can be read as a story). When writing was invented the floodgates were opened. Amongst the preserved ruins of Pompeii (destroyed in 79 AD by the volcano, Vesuvius) hundreds of examples of graffiti were found. This is a typical example:

"Chius, I hope your piles are chafed once more, that they may burn worse than they burnt before."

Other graffiti complained about the government.

In the Middle Ages in Britain, graffiti was most commonly found, written in Latin, on church walls. "Death is like a shadow which always follows the body" is a typically cheerful example. During the Seventeenth and Eighteenth Centuries the graffiti was mostly rude. Here is just about the cleanest example:

"Clarinda lay here
with a young cavalier,
with her heart full of fear,
for her husband was near."
L.L. 2 February 1728

Mysteriously, graffiti died out completely during Victorian times. It became popular again in the 'thirties, and it was at this time that the craze for badges (walking graffiti) began.

I'm looking for a thrill

was one daring example.

During the Second World War, the legendary character, Kilroy, appeared. "Kilroy was here" has been found, over the years, written at the top of the Statue of Liberty, the base of the Marco Polo bridge in China, and under the Arc de Triomphe in Paris! By the end of the 1960s, sometimes called 'The Age of Protest', graffiti of a very political nature had begun to appear, particularly in America during the Vietnam war, where examples like these were very common:

"God is not on our side."

"War is good business – invest your sons."

"Guns don't kill people – people kill people."

In recent times, graffiti has earned respectability in some areas. In Stockholm, for example, there is a graffiti wall provided for members of the public. Every night it is painted over, allowing would-be scribblers to start afresh the next morning. In America, and increasingly in Europe, some forms are regarded as art. But many people regard the vast majority of graffiti as unsightly and meaningless. What do you think?

Options

● Discuss in your groups what sort of people 'do' graffiti.

● What do you think of these definitions?
"Dirty words on clean walls."
"A dialogue between an anonymous individual and the world."

● Try and work out your own definition. Collect and analyse examples of graffiti in your local school, community, town. Decide which are:
1. just gossip,
2. to make people laugh,
3. done in anger,
4. with passion,
5. political,
6. declarations of love,
7. of the 'I was here' kind.

● Sometimes graffiti can be very sinister. Write a story which ends with the sentence:
"When the door was opened they found the words — scrawled across the wall."

● With a partner examine the newspaper article.

● Write a letter to the local newspaper, criticising mural projects. Use a phrase condemning graffiti as your heading. Your partner could then write the reply, again selecting an appropriate heading.

Going to the Wall

Kilroy hasn't been to Sheffield for years but his spirit lives on in the subways and suburbs where the moving hand has created a sociologists' paradise. Some call it art, but for the city council it has become a recurring nightmare.

Council-led initiatives to outlaw graffiti in city-centre subways have consistently met with failure, but one Sheffield school has been successfully breaking down the boundaries between graffiti and art through a series of mural projects in the surrounding community.

Herries School, in Hillsborough, is one of those red-brick and concrete flat-roofed functional products of post-war austerity architecture, a social priority school in the middle of a large council estate.

When headmaster Mr. Giles Pepper arrived five years ago he entered a typical blackboard jungle with stark, featureless corridors and uninviting classrooms. He and his staff began gradually to introduce the concept of community education. The school was opened for other uses outside curriculum hours, children were consulted about their environment.

Deputy Headmaster, Mr. Graham Evans, said: "They wanted simple additions, curtains at the windows, plants in the corridors, display cases, seats, and large colourful paintings. Nobody had bothered to ask them before."

Art teacher Mr. Chris Iredale introduced his fifth form pupils to mural painting as part of the new policy. Wall paintings started to appear in the drab corridors and the work has now spread extra-mural to the school outfields and into one of the more depressing suburban areas.

"The noticeable thing about the brighter corridors and the murals is that they have not been seriously vandalised. The children seem to care for them," said Mr. Evans. What, no graffiti? Very little, certainly none of the aerosol-daubed slogans that have become all too familiar in the inner-cities. At least that was the case until last week.

Pupils under Mr. Iredale's guidance had painted a giant 40-feet-long mural of a train stretching the length of a concrete-clad hut. Mr. Evans said: "Our own kids are proud of the work and wouldn't dream of writing on it, but a gang of older youths got into the grounds and covered it with its own slogans."

The gang which has plastered the apparently-meaningless phrase "Sin 6 FBI" on walls, lamp-posts, houses and bridges throughout the Hillsborough area is one more example of the graffiti writer's obsession which continues to defy explanation.

"We clamp down on that sort of thing straight away," said Graham Evans. "We have to ask ourselves what is and what is not acceptable, and that certainly is not. I questioned one girl at the school why she had written some graffiti in the toilets. 'Would you do it in your own home?' I asked, and she replied that her father allowed her to do so as long as it was confined to the lavatory wall.

"We noticed one phenomenon about lavatory graffiti. It is far more abusive, sexist, violent and explicit in the girls' toilets than it ever is in the boys. But just why it appears I don't know. Kids go to extraordinary lengths. They will walk miles to write on a blank wall. They will even hang over a road bridge with friends holding their legs."

Richard Donkin, *The Yorkshire Post*, 16 October 1986

One of the strange things about graffiti is that it is incredibly rare to catch someone doing it!

Options

● Select one of the following situations and construct a roleplay around it.
1. A council official catches someone spraying their name on a public building.
2. A teacher confronts a pupil writing a piece of racist graffiti on the back of a book.
3. A passer-by sees someone writing political graffiti on a wall. (The passer-by can have the same or opposing political views, but must nonetheless disagree with graffiti.)
4. A local resident comes out of his/her house to complain about a mural project that is just being started on a wall across the road.

● Is it art? Is it an eyesore? Is it both? Write an article for a teenage magazine on the subject. (Use *Repromaster 40* to improve the presentation of your article). Your list of points from the article above, for and against, may be useful. What is your attitude to graffiti artists?

VARIATIONS

Words, Words, Words

We don't speak of tribal wars anymore
we say simply faction fights
there are no tribes around here
only nations
it makes sense you see
'cause from there
one moves to multinational
it makes sense you get me
'cause from there
one gets one's homeland
which is a reasonable idea
'cause from there
one can dabble with independence
which deserves warm applause
– the bloodless revolution

we are talking of words
words tossed around as if
denied location by the wind
we mean those words some spit
others grab
dress them up for the occasion
fling them on the lap of an audience
we are talking of those words
that stalk our lives like policemen
words no dictionary can embrace
words that change sooner than seasons
we mean words
that spell out our lives
words, words, words
for there's a kind of poetic licence
doing the rounds in these parts.
Sipho Sepamla

"I don't know what you mean by 'glory'," Alice said.

Humpty Dumpty smiled contemptuously. "Of course you don't – till I tell you. I meant 'there's a nice knock-down argument for you.'"

"But 'glory' doesn't mean 'a nice knockdown argument'," Alice objected.

"When *I* use a word," Humpty Dumpty said in rather a scornful tone, "it means just what I choose it to mean – neither more nor less."

"The question is," said Alice, "whether you *can* make words mean so many different things."

"The question is," said Humpty Dumpty, "which is to be master – that's all."

Alice was too much puzzled to say anything, so, after a minute, Humpty Dumpty began again. "They've a temper, some of them – particularly verbs, they're the proudest. Adjectives you can do anything with, but not verbs. However, *I* can manage the whole lot of them! Impenetrability! That's what *I* say!"

"Would you tell me, please," said Alice, "what that means?"

"Now you talk like a reasonable child," said Humpty Dumpty, looking very much pleased. "I meant by 'impenetrability' that we've had enough of that subject, and it would be just as well if you'd mention what you mean to do next, as I suppose you don't mean to stop here all the rest of your life."

"That's a great deal to make one word mean," Alice said in a thoughtful tone.

"When I make a word do a lot of work like that," said Humpty Dumpty, "I always pay it extra."

"Oh!" said Alice. She was too much puzzled to make any other remark.

"Ah, you should see 'em come round me of a Saturday night," Humpty Dumpty went on, wagging his head gravely from side to side; "for to get their wages."
Lewis Carroll, *Alice Through the Looking Glass*

The Ad-man

This trumpeter of nothingness, employed
To keep our reason full and null and void:
This man of wind and froth and flux will sell
The wares of any who reward him well,
Praising whatever he is paid to praise,
He hunts for ever-newer, smarter ways
To make the gilt seem gold; the shoddy, silk;
To cheat us legally; to bluff and bilk
By methods which no jury can prevent
Because the law's not broken, only bent.

This mind for hire, this mental prostitute
Can tell the half-lie hardest to refute;
Knows how to hide an inconvenient fact
And when to leave a doubtful claim unbacked;
Manipulates the truth, but not too much,
And if his patter needs the Human Touch
Then aptly artless, artfully naive,
He wears his fickle heart upon his sleeve.

He takes ideas and trains them to engage
In the long little wars big combines wage.
He keeps his logic loose, his feelings flimsy;
Turns eloquence to cant and wit to whimsy;
Trims language till it fits his client's pattern,
And style's a glossy tart or limping slattern.

He uses words that once were strong and fine.
Primal as sun and moon and bread and wine,
True, honourable, honoured, clear and clean,
And leaves them shabby, worn, diminished, mean.
A. S. J. Tessimond

Bomb Commercials
(for two voices)

1 A. Get PAD nuclear meat for humans
  B. Don't give your family ordinary meat, give them PAD
  A. P.A.D. – Prolongs Active Death
  B. Enriched with nourishing marrowbone strontium.

2 A. All over the world, more and more people are changing to
BOMB
  B. BOMB – The International passport to smoking ruins

3 B. . . . *so then I said 'well lets all go for a picnic and we went and it was all right except for a bit of sand in the butties and then of course the wasps and Michael fell in the river but what I say is you can't have everything perfect can you so just then there was a big bang and the whole place caught fire and something happened to Michael's arms and I don't know what happened to my Hubby and its perhaps as well as there were only four pieces of Kit-Kat so we had one each and then we had to walk home 'cos there weren't any buses . . .*
  A. HAVE A BREAK – HAVE A KIT-KAT

4 A. Everyday in cities all over England people are breathing in Fall-out
  B. Get the taste of the Bomb out of your mouth with OVAL FRUITS

5 A. General Howard J. Sherman has just pressed the button that killed 200 million people. A BIG job with BIG responsibilities. The General has to decide between peace and the extinction of the human race . . .
  B. But he can't tell Stork from Butter.
Adrian Henri

ACKNOWLEDGEMENTS

Unit 1

Page 8: surnames reflecting medieval life from *The Guinness Book of Names*, published by Guinness Publishing Ltd. Place names from *Let's Use the Locality* by Henry Pluckrose, published by Unwin Hyman. **Page 10:** extract from *Kes* © Barry Hines and Allan Stronach 1976, reproduced by permission of Curtis Brown Ltd. Extract from *A Kestrel for a Knave* by Barry Hines, published by Michael Joseph Ltd. **Page 17:** Extremely Repulsive Thing Carrier and Low Flying Bird Destroyer from *The Cycle, a Catalogue* by Wilf Lunn. **Page 19:** *Words* by Edward Thomas from *The Collected Poems of Edward Thomas*, published by Oxford University Press, reproduced by permission of Myfanwy Thomas. *Epilogue* by Grace Nicols from *I is a Long-memoried Woman*, published by Karnac House. *Word* by Stephen Spender, reproduced by permission of Faber and Faber Ltd. from *Collected Poems* by Stephen Spender.

Unit 2

Page 22: *Baby Song* by Thom Gunn, reprinted by permission of Faber and Faber Ltd. from *Jack Straw's Castle* by Thom Gunn. **Page 26:** table of early reading words from *Key Words to Literacy*, published by The Teacher Publishing Company Ltd. **Page 27:** *Reading Scheme* by Wendy Cope reprinted by permission of Faber and Faber Ltd. from *Making Cocoa for Kingsley Amis* by Wendy Cope. **Page 28, 29:** 2 extracts from *How Green You Are* by Berlie Doherty, published by Methuen Children's Books. Extract from *Nemesis* by Agatha Christie, © Agatha Christie Ltd. 1971. **Page 30, 31, 32:** extracts from *Under the Eye of the Clock* by Christopher Nolan, published by George Weidenfeld & Nicolson Ltd. **Page 36:** passage by Wai Keung, from *Many Voices*, published by Routledge. **Page 37:** *Unsaid* by John La Rose, from *News for Babylon* published by Chatto and Windus. **Page 39:** *No Rain, No Rainbow* by John Agard, from *Say It Again, Granny!* illustrated by Susanna Gretz, published by The Bodley Head. *Parents' Sayings* by Michael Rosen, from *When Did You Last Wash Your Feet?* published by André Deutsch Ltd. **Page 41:** extract from *Body Language* by Gordon Wainwright, published by Hodder & Stoughton. **Page 42:** extract from *Animal Farm* by George Orwell, reprinted by permission of the Estate of the late Sonia Brownell Orwell and Martin Secker & Warburg. **Page 43:** *Killing a Whale* by David Gill, from *The Pagoda* published by Chatto & Windus. **Page 46:** *Morning Song* by Sylvia Plath, from *Collected Poems by Sylvia Plath*, published by Faber and Faber Ltd., © Ted Hughes 1965 & 1981, reprinted by permission of Olwyn Hughes. **Page 47:** *Slow Reader* © Vicki Feaver. Poem © Su Andi. *Poem for a Dead Poet* by Roger McGough from *Holiday on Death Row* published by Jonathan Cape Ltd.

Unit 3

Page 50: extract from *The Roads* by Padraic Pearse, from *Short Stories by Padraic Pearse*, selected and adapted by Desmond Maguire, published by The Mercier Press. Extract from *William Williams Pantycelyn* by J. Gwilym Jones, published by the University of Wales Press. **Page 51:** extract from *Beowulf*, edited and translated by Michael Swanton, published by Manchester University Press. **Page 52:** extract from *Chaucer's Canterbury Tales* edited by A. Kent Hieatt and Constance Hieatt, published by Bantam Books. **Page 54:** extract from *Enthusiasms* by Bernard Levin, published by Jonathan Cape Ltd. **Page 57:** cartoon *There, Their, They're* reproduced by permission of Nigel Paige. **Page 58:** *According to My Mood* ©

Benjamin Zephaniah. **Page 59:** extract from *Interpungendi Ratio* by Aldus Manutius, from the translation in *Punctuation, its Principles and Practice* by T.F. and M.F.A. Husband, published by Routledge. **Page 60:** extracts by Shiranikha Herbert and Leonard Barden from *The Guardian* 29 October 1988. **Page 61:** Sony Walkman instructions reproduced by permission of Sony U.K. Ltd. **Page 62:** *The Do-It-Yourself Lakeland Multiple Choice Postcard* reproduced by permission of Cardtoons Publications Ltd. Extract from *Nineteen Eighty-four* by George Orwell reprinted by permission of the Estate of the late Sonia Brownell Orwell and Martin Secker & Warburg. **Page 63:** *Constancy* by Choshu from *An Introduction to Haiku* by Harold G. Henderson, © 1958 by Harold G. Henderson, reprinted by permission of Doubleday, a division of Bantam, Doubleday, Dell publishing group, Inc. *The Reason of Man and the Instinct of the Beast* by Jonathan Stoker, and *Converted* by Jack Union, from *The Book of Mini-Sagas II*, published by Alan Sutton Publishing Ltd., Gloucester, © Telegraph Sunday Magazine. **Page 64:** extract from *Parlez-Vous Franglais* by Miles Kington, published by Robson Books Ltd. Extract from *The Story of English* by Robert McCrum, William Cran and Robert MacNeil, reproduced with the permission of BBC Enterprises Ltd. **Page 66:** extract from *Developing Reading 3-13* by Roger Beard, published by Hodder & Stoughton. *Silly Norman* by John Lennon, from *Spaniard in the Works*, published by Jonathan Cape Ltd., reprinted by permission of the Estate of John Lennon and Jonathan Cape Ltd. **Page 68:** *Gust Becos I Cud Not Spel* by Alan Ahlberg from *Gargling With Jelly* by Brian Patten, published by Kestrel Books 1985, reproduced by permission of Penguin Books Ltd. *Typewriting Class* by Gareth Owen, from *Song of the City*, published by Collins. **Page 69:** *A Good English Recipe* by Linda Dowse, from *Worlds Apart*, published by Mary Glasgow Publications Ltd., London. *Writing* © Jan Dean. *Private? No!* by Willard R. Espy, from *Another Almanac of Words at Play*, published by André Deutsch Ltd.

Unit 4

Page 75: Letter to parents from *Linking Home and School: A New Review* by Craft, Raynor and Cohen, published by Harper & Row. **Page 79:** *Jacko Wows 'em at Wembley* by Rick Sky, from *The Sun*, 15 July 1988. **Page 80:** *The Greatest Showman* by Adam Sweeting, from *The Guardian*, 16 July 1988. **Page 81:** *Naming of Parts* by Henry Reed, from *A Map of Verona*, published by Jonathan Cape Ltd., reprinted by permission of the Estate of Henry Reed and Jonathan Cape Ltd. **Page 82:** extract from *Roll of Thunder, Hear My Cry* by Mildred Taylor, published by Victor Gollancz Ltd. **Page 84:** extract from *The Complete Plain Words* by Sir Ernest Gowers, reproduced by permission of the Controller of Her Majesty's Stationery Office. **Page 86:** *Horror Film* by Gareth Owen, from *Song of the City*, published by Collins. **Page 87:** *A Word in Edgeways* by Charles Tomlinson, reprinted from Charles Tomlinson's *Collected Poems* (1985) by permission of Oxford University Press.

Unit 5

Page 90: extract from *Accent, Dialect and the School* by Peter Trudgill, published by Edward Arnold. **Page 91:** *Speech Communities* by Madeleine Rock, from *Say What You Think*, published by The English Centre. **Page 92, 93:** *Goldilocks and the Three Bears* from *The Queen's English* by Dorgan Rushton, published by Michael Joseph Ltd. **Page 94:** article on slang by Robert McCrum, from *The Listener*, 9 October 1986.